SPEAKING
THE MODI WAY

Virender Kapoor is a thinker, an educationist and an inspirational guru. An alumnus of IIT Bombay and the former director of a prestigious management institute under the Symbiosis umbrella, he is the co-founder of Orange Ivy playschools, Pune. His books on emotional intelligence, leadership and self-help have been translated into several regional and foreign languages. To know more about him, log on to www.virenderkapoor.com or mail him at virenderkapoor21@yahoo.com

Other books in the series:
Leadership: The Gandhi Way
Innovation: The Einstein Way

SPEAKING
THE MODI WAY

VIRENDER KAPOOR

Published by
Rupa Publications India Pvt. Ltd 2016
7/16, Ansari Road, Daryaganj
New Delhi 110002

Sales centres:
Allahabad Bengaluru Chennai
Hyderabad Jaipur Kathmandu
Kolkata Mumbai

Copyright © Virender Kapoor 2016

The views and opinions expressed in this book are the author's
own and the facts are as reported by him/her which have been
verified to the extent possible, and the publishers
are not in any way liable for the same.

All rights reserved.

No part of this publication may be reproduced, transmitted,
or stored in a retrieval system, in any form or by any means,
electronic, mechanical, photocopying, recording or otherwise,
without the prior permission of the publisher.

ISBN: 978-81-291-3969-6

First impression 2016

10 9 8 7 6 5 4 3 2 1

The moral right of the author has been asserted.

Typeset by SÜRYA, New Delhi
Printed at Gopsons Papers Ltd., Noida

This book is sold subject to the condition that it shall not,
by way of trade or otherwise, be lent, resold, hired out,
or otherwise circulated, without the publisher's
prior consent, in any form of binding or cover
other than that in which it is published.

CONTENTS

PREFACE — vii

PRELUDE — xi
From Chaiwala to Chancellor

1. SINCERITY OF PURPOSE AND FOCUSED APPROACH — 1
   Floating like a Butterfly, Stinging like a Bee

2. A SPARTAN SOLDIER — 12
   Self-discipline, Spirituality and Simplicity

3. DIFFERENT AUDIENCE, DIFFERENT STROKES — 20
   Speaking from the Heart

4. FACTS AT YOUR FINGERTIPS — 39
   Develop the Art of Using Logic to Convey Your Vision

5. BECOME A GRANDMASTER — 60
   Stories, Similes, Slogans and Rhetoric

6. FEROCITY OF HOPE — 81
   Philosophy. Strategy. Action. Simplicity

CONTENTS

7. USING THE PAST TO INSPIRE THE FUTURE — 100
   *History. Histrionics. Humour. Mythology.
   Common Sense. Culture*

8. STOP ME IF YOU CAN — 110
   Packaging Ideas and Presenting Them Effectively

9. FIRST AMONGST EQUALS — 116
   Creating a Unique Lexicon

10. THE POWER OF THE SPOKEN WORD — 126
    The Art of Influencing People

PREFACE

'He came, he spoke, he conquered.'

—An adaptation of Julius Caesar's immortal words 'Veni, vidi, vici'
(I came, I saw, I conquered)

On 13 September 2013, Narendra Damodardas Modi appeared on the national arena as the prime ministerial candidate of the Bharatiya Janata Party (BJP). Not many outside Gujarat knew of this state chief minister (CM) who had been voted to power in four consecutive elections and had held office for twelve years in succession. Now, with barely six months in hand before the country went to the polls in April 2014, Modi had the arduous task of reaching out to India's 1.25 billion people spread across twenty-nine states and seven union territories.

As the prime ministerial candidate he travelled extensively, addressing millions through hundreds of rallies. His words and vision combined the best of rhetoric with substance, motivating and mesmerizing young and old. He not only delivered brilliant speeches consistently, but improved upon each.

His campaign will go down as one of the most effective in Indian history. His victory did not stem, as had Obama's, from one brilliant and rousing speech (Obama's keynote address at the 2004 Democratic National Convention) that electrified America. Modi's was a steadier, more consistent, ever-improving performance, where audiences waited in awe to listen, expecting him to say something different each time—and he did not disappoint them. For the people of India, as regards Modi, it was always '*Yeh dil maange more*'.

Modi is also among those few leaders globally who has maintained an ongoing dialogue with the people after being sworn in as prime minister. Most leaders don't think it necessary to address the people as frequently once they get the top job; the majority get bogged down by the daily routine and find little time to connect.

Modi did it differently—he wanted to remain connected with the people and managed to do so. As prime minister, he relied on his brilliant oratorical skills to convey not only his vision, his modus operandi and mission, but also to motivate the Indian masses who had almost lost hope and had little faith in the political class. He fully understood that in order to mobilize the nation he had to share his vision and aspirations with the people from day one.

He adopted a three-pronged strategy—address the people, address those that make up the machinery of the government and address nations and people abroad who matter. He kept at it, again improving with every speech, springing surprise after surprise with his brilliantly crafted speeches each time he spoke.

Abroad he has been called a 'rock star', and is seen as a charismatic, original, authentic, energizing, inspiring and even compelling leader. There is no doubt that he has emerged as one of the world's most accomplished speakers.

How has this man accomplished all this in such a short period? What quality is it that makes people look up to him? What communication strategy and practices have enabled him to move rapidly from near obscurity to being hailed as one of the most brilliant speakers in the world? And can we learn to become better speakers by understanding this master orator? These are the questions that prompted me to write this book.

Speaking: The Modi Way focuses on those techniques used by Narendra Modi that make him such a great orator. If we analyse his speeches so far, we find that they not only reflect his role as a leader, but on several occasions, his role as a mentor, visionary and teacher too—as though he wears different hats on different occasions.

The manner in which he changes his substance, his content, his body language, his examples, his stories, his tone, his pace and his pitch according to the audience is something that intrigues most people. Thus, as mentioned earlier, every speech appears to be different. He comes across as genuine and honest, speaking from the heart and connecting with each member of the audience—something we need to learn from this master craftsman. How does he manage such a mammoth stage presence, how does he address such disparate segments of society at one go, yet reach out to each; how does he inspire the ordinary man, the scientist, the intellectual, the economist, the industrialist, the student and the teacher?

Narendra Modi is a game changer who has followed in the footsteps of former Prime Minister Atal Bihari Vajpayee. He has demonstrated to the metro-based middle classes that you don't need English to deliver a brilliant oratorical performance. He has addressed NASSCOM[1], school and college students, as well as Indians abroad in Hindi, and to thunderous applause.

---

[1]National Association of Software and Services Companies (NASSCOM) is a trade association of the Indian information technology (IT) and the business process outsourcing (BPO) industry.

Just as music breaks language barriers, Modi has established that language is no barrier to great oratory.

I have examined every facet of this enigmatic orator layer by layer and tried to distil every ounce of wisdom from some of his most brilliant speeches. I have tried to dissect his art of persuasion, his nuances and his ability to connect and convince audience members as young as ten and as old as eighty. No other prime minister in the history of modern India has created disciples—Modi doesn't just have fans, he has millions of 'Modi bhakts'.

Speaking: The Modi Way lays bare all of these fascinating facts and much more. It analyses and draws lessons which can be used by leaders in institutions—whether business, non-profit or academic—and in daily life. The insights provided by this book can also be gainfully used by students, managers and professionals. This book lays the foundation for mastering the art of persuasion and the power of rhetoric, and will prove to be of immense use to people who want to improve their communication skills.

Oratory cannot exist in a void. Modi's oratory occurs in the context of leadership. Therefore, this book also covers the leadership and personality traits of Narendra Modi.

Ultimately, a good speaker must attain the highest level of proficiency to become an orator, becoming someone who can convince and persuade his audience whenever he or she rises to speak. *Speaking: The Modi Way* shows you the way.

PRELUDE

From Chaiwala to Chancellor

'A dream doesn't become reality through magic; it takes sweat, determination and hard work.'
—Colin Powell

From Humble Beginnings

Narendra Modi was born on 17 September 1950 in Vadnagar, Gujarat, to a family that belonged to the Ghanchi Teli ('Oil Worker') community, categorized as Other Backward Classes (OBC) in the Constitution of India. His father, Damodardas Mulchand Modi, ran a small grocery shop while mother Heeraben Modi was a housewife who looked after her home and six children—Narendra was her third child. The family lived in a three-roomed house that had no toilet or bathing facility. Drinking water was fetched from a nearby well and the boys and their father bathed in a lake. As the family grew, Damodardas Modi built an additional floor with tin-sheet roofing.

Young Narendra Modi was a bright student who had the knack of making friends easily. He got on well with his classmates and the other children in his locality and had a large circle of friends. He is also said to have never picked a fight with his brothers and sisters. Keeping mum in the face of disagreements was apparently his way of protesting.

He also developed a love for reading early on. An inquisitive and intelligent child, he did well in Social Studies and English at school. He spent a lot of his free time at the town library, engrossed in children's magazines and comics. Some of his mentors gifted him books that he liked, because they knew he would love them. He also saved to buy books and eventually built his own little library. As he grew older, books by Swami Vivekananda inspired him—he was tremendously influenced by the latter's political thought, patriotism and spirituality. In later years Modi's spiritual quest, his yearning for truth, would take him to the spiritual centres and ashrams that he had read about in Vivekananda's books. It would also not be wrong to say that Modi's early love of reading helped build his intellect and provided him a solid base upon which to build his oratorical skills. As a young boy, he actively participated in debates at school, and teachers as well as fellow classmates appreciated his clarity of thought and his views on the topics being debated.

Modi demonstrated a great sense of right and wrong early on, even if it meant speaking up in front of the school principal. It is said that he once saw a few classmates beating up a fellow student, and quickly squirted ink on the shirts of the perpetrators. When the principal learnt about the beating, he personally visited the class and asked the bullies to stand up. No one stood up, until young Modi told the principal that the culprits had ink on their shirts and then they were punished.

Another incident worth narrating is about how young Modi dug in his heels and refused to obey his teacher's order that all homework would henceforth be corrected by the class monitor. Modi was clear that his homework would be corrected by his teacher, and nobody else. Clearly, young Modi held firm to his opinions and beliefs. Once he made up his mind he would not budge, and was forthright about his opinion—in that sense, he could even be considered outspoken. However, such rebellion was rarely seen; he was normally very respectful and always ready to volunteer for any additional work that his teachers assigned to him.

Spirit of Service

This attitude of helpfulness extended to the home front too—Modi's father started a tea stall where the young boy willingly lent a hand after school hours. He also readily helped his mother with household chores and sometimes volunteered to cook for the family. A strong inclination to serve, coupled with an equally strong patriotic fervour, led Narendra Modi to join the Rashtriya Swayamsevak Sangh (RSS) shakha in his hometown at the age of eight. However, he would work equally enthusiastically for a Congress function as he would for the RSS or the Bharatiya Jana Sangh. That childlike enthusiasm is intact in him even today. He also wanted to join the army, but his father was against this.

As a child of parents with limited means, Modi also learnt the value of frugality early on. He is said to have had only two sets of clothes, but made sure they were well maintained, so that he looked neatly turned out.

Spiritual and Physical Courage

Not only did Modi display the courage of conviction, he also displayed physical courage. He was fond of swimming in a nearby lake which had a small island, on which stood a temple with a flag at its pinnacle. This flag was brought down and a special flag hoisted on auspicious days and religious occasions. Devotees would volunteer for this task. On one such occasion, however, it had rained heavily and the lake was flooded. Swimming to the island would not be easy. Crocodiles had also surfaced because of the rising water. Modi, who was just a twelve-year-old, volunteered along with a couple of equally brave young friends, swam across, changed the flag and swam back.

Modi's family was very religious and had dedicated one room to the gods even in their small house, where a small temple housed the family deity and other idols. Other than regular prayers with the family, Modi also developed the habit of visiting a nearby temple. His pursuit of spirituality was inspired by Swami Vivekananda, and self-denial and self-discipline marked his character. He observed the Navratri fast twice a year and thus developed the habit of renunciation very early. He gave up eating salt, jaggery, chillies and oily food. Despite a punishing near-eighteen-hour schedule as prime minister, he has kept his habit of fasting intact to this day.

Fasting is a spiritual exercise that engenders the development of strong willpower and the spirit of regimentation. It has another, deeper purpose—if you can say no to good food and are able to take hunger pangs in your stride, you will be able to say no to a bribe, no to lust, no to lethargy and even no to flattery.

A Great Organizer

In a TV interview in 2015, Modi said that the capability to organize and get things done was God's gift to him. At the age of nine, employing drive, initiative and determination, he organized a food stall with his friends, the proceeds of which went towards relief efforts following the flooding of the Tapi River. He knew how to motivate friends to volunteer for a cause, how to organize an event that would generate a viable income to fund a project. Once, he organized a play at school with his friends to raise funds for a wall to be built around the school. The play was a success and the sum collected surpassed the expectations of his friends and teachers.

As an educationist, I have observed over a period of time that MBA students, who volunteer to work for the batch and for the college by participating in activities through student committees, do well in their career in later years. Modi kept up volunteer work throughout his growing years. In 1967, at the age of seventeen, he worked for flood relief, serving the flood-affected across Gujarat. He served tea to jawans at the railway station during the 1965 India–Pakistan war. He has always displayed a spirit of service towards fellow countrymen and those in need.

In Search of Truth

After a year in college Modi decided to quit studies and set off in search of truth. Books had led him to spirituality, but now he wanted to acquire hands-on spiritual knowledge. He left home with very little money and for almost two years remained out of touch with his parents, friends and family, travelling to ashrams founded by Swami Vivekananda. He sought to join the Belur Math near Kolkata, but was turned away because he was underage.

Not many details are known about how he spent these two

years, other than the fact that he travelled across the country visiting ashrams in the north and northeastern India and getting familiar with the day-to-day life and learning of the monks. He visited the hill station of Almora to stay at the Advaita Ashram there. At Rajkot he spent a considerable time at the Ramakrishna Mission.

Returning home after two years, he spent just a few days with his mother before moving to Ahmedabad, where he stayed with his uncle and began working at his canteen at the Gujarat State Road Transport Corporation. Then twenty, Modi was still a rolling stone, looking for something without knowing what he was looking for.

The Calling

While working at his uncle's canteen he continued attending spiritual meetings and political debates, and by 1972 decided to join the RSS full time. A devout Hindu, he was impressed by the dedication and discipline of the RSS cadres. He renewed contact with Lakshmanrao Inamdar, who had inducted him into the RSS as a Bal Swayamsevak (child volunteer) when he was eight years old. Inamdar, popularly called Vakil Sahib, was thereafter instrumental in training and grooming Modi as an intern in the RSS.

Modi then left his uncle's home and moved into the Inamdar home, which had around fifteen people. He pitched in with the daily chores, starting his day early—fetching milk and making tea for everybody before attending the shakha; returning in time to make breakfast for all, before cleaning and sweeping the house and washing his clothes.

He came into contact with many people there, including

Eknath Ranade who had established the Vivekananda rock memorial at Kanyakumari. As time went on he was asked to play a bigger role within the RSS and was given more responsibility, being asked to look after the RSS's office correspondence, spanning certain regions. Later, he was asked to organize the logistics for swayamsevaks and their families who visited Ahmedabad for medical treatment, or for attending RSS meetings. In addition, he managed the travel arrangements of those members who had to undertake tours to various parts of Gujarat. Gradually emerging as one of the most trusted and dependable Sangh workers, Modi earned respect for his hard work, selfless approach and never-say-die attitude. He was a real grass-roots worker and connected with people from all walks of life.

Inamdar, meanwhile, motivated Modi to go for higher studies. And so Modi enrolled at Delhi University and obtained a Bachelor's degree in Political Science before going on to do his Master's in Political Science from the University of Gujarat.

A True Workaholic

Narendra Modi is a workaholic, as became evident to his mentors early on, in the RSS and later in the BJP. He enjoyed work, and looked upon every type of work as a learning experience—a winner's attitude. Whatever the quantum, he not only knew how to attract more work and get things done, but did so with enthusiasm, throwing his entire might behind it. This is a great leadership trait, but one that very few leaders actually have. It is one thing to give orders and entirely another to roll up your sleeves and get into battle mode yourself. Modi always leads from the front. Even before he had formally joined the RSS he had participated in several movements, such as that for 'Gau Raksha' (cow protection), and in an agitation against price rise.

In 1972, Gujarat was grappling with severe drought and famine, which led to an uprising led by Jayaprakash Narayan against the Congress government in the state. The government faced severe criticism for not handling the famine properly, and students and the middle class launched a movement called the 'Navnirman Andolan' against price rise. By the end of 1973 the movement had turned into a call for total revolution and non-cooperation with the government. Modi was impressed by Jayaprakash Narayan's personality and his philosophy. The RSS supported this movement and the revolution got further momentum, eventually toppling the Congress government in the state.

Indira Gandhi clamped Emergency on the nation on 26 June 1975. All opposition leaders were arrested, including Atal Bihari Vajpayee, Lal Krishna Advani, Jayaprakash Narayan and Morarji Desai. The RSS decided that its workers would work underground, staying in safe houses to avoid being arrested by the police. The party cadres would strictly follow non-violent resistance. Narendra Modi, barely three years into full-time RSS activities, got a taste of political upheaval that was to push him into national-level politics very soon.

Role During the Emergency

The Emergency was lifted on 22 March 1977 after twenty-one months. This was a very tough period for the Jan Sangh and the RSS, and twenty-five-year-old Narendra Modi was in the thick of it. He had proven himself to be dependable and responsible and displayed great organizational acumen. Now that the government had banned the RSS, and RSS cadres had to go underground, Modi was made responsible for looking after the swayamsevaks and arranging safe accommodation for them. He was also tasked with the printing of booklets and leaflets as well as their optimal distribution. An international conference was held in Delhi by the central government during this period, and the RSS wanted to send a message to the delegates. Modi, in a clandestine operation, got five different booklets published and managed to dispatch them by train.

He was also responsible for organizing meetings of RSS workers and other Sangh Parivar leaders during this time. To avoid arrest by the police, he sometimes disguised himself as a sanyasi and sometimes grew a beard and donned a turban, disguising himself as a Sikh. But Modi's toughest task was to organize funds for the party to continue its struggle and support the families of those who were jailed. The rich were scared to donate, since the government was keeping a strict watch on all their activities. Modi used every source that he could tap—common men and women, shop-owners and workers. The amounts were small but this was the best way for him to fund the movement.

Underground workers met secretly at different levels of the RSS and Jana Sangh hierarchy. Modi also got an opportunity to meet leaders from other political parties, like George Fernandes, Raj Narain and Charan Singh. Nevertheless, for him, this remained a period of struggle and learning.

Rise Within the Party

Within a year of the Emergency being lifted, Narendra Modi was made 'Vibhag Pradhan' or departmental head with six districts under him. In a couple of years he was promoted to the position of 'Prant Padadhikari' or regional head, as well as made the joint president of the RSS's regional organizations. By now he had won the hearts and minds of not only his colleagues but also of his bosses in the Sangh Parivar. And he was just thirty-one years old.

Electoral Politics

In 1985 Modi moved from the RSS to the BJP, the political party mentored by the RSS, and within three years was elected as organizing secretary of the BJP's Gujarat unit. In 1990 he was picked up by L.K. Advani for his Ayodhya Rath Yatra on the basis of his strong organizational skills and proven ability to deliver results. Later he helped Murli Manohar Joshi during his Ekta Yatra in 1991–92. This was the time when the central leadership identified his great potential.

Thereafter he was instrumental in the BJP's 1995 win in the Gujarat state assembly elections. By November 1995 he had been elected as the BJP national secretary and moved to Delhi, where he became a part of mainstream politics. He was also given charge of the party's campaign machinery in the 1999 Lok Sabha elections in Gujarat. He did a commendable job by motivating the RSS, BJP and Vishwa Hindu Parishad (VHP) workers, and the BJP won 20 out of 26 seats.

By 2001, BJP Chief Minister (CM) in Gujarat Keshubhai Patel developed health problems and also lost ground politically because he had been unable to manage the political fallout of the post-2001 earthquake period. The BJP's national leadership had to seriously think of replacing him and there was a hunt for a new candidate. Modi's name came up for consideration.

Advani and several others were of the opinion that Modi lacked experience and proposed that he be made Deputy CM and assist Patel. Modi declined and told Atal Bihari Vajpayee that he would either be fully responsible for Gujarat or not at all. The central leadership decided to make him CM and he replaced Keshubhai Patel on 3 October 2001.

In his first term as CM, he was put to a severe test of ability and creditability. On 27 February 2002, within months of taking over, Godhra happened. Over sixty people were killed when a train coming from Ayodhya was burnt at Godhra. The incident sparked a Hindu–Muslim riot that led to an estimated 900 to 2,000 dead and an equal number injured. As is very well known, the Modi government was criticized for not handling the riots effectively and Modi was accused of not taking sufficient action against the rioters. Many political parties that were a part of the National Democratic Alliance (NDA) government at the centre, and those in the opposition, wanted Modi to resign. Modi submitted his resignation, which was turned down by the central BJP leadership. The official term of the assembly was to end by December 2002 and Gujarat went for assembly elections again. BJP, under Modi's leadership, won 127 seats out of 182 and Modi was sworn in as CM for his second term.

This time, his agenda was economic development and overall progress of the state. He encouraged privatization, invited investors and worked towards a corruption-free state. He came up with out-of-the-box solutions and started a biennial investors' summit called 'Vibrant Gujarat'. In the first summit held in 2003, seventy-six memoranda of understanding (MOUs) worth USD 14 billion were signed.

Completing a successful second term in Gujarat, Modi

again took the BJP to victory, with the party winning 117 seats in the assembly elections. In his third term as chief minister, Modi's entire focus was on full-scale development to build a vibrant Gujarat. Semi-arid and not known for an active agrarian economy, Gujarat underwent a major change under Modi. By end-2008, 500,000 structures and check dams had been built—ten times more than the number constructed in the last forty years. This helped counter erosion and raised the water table across the state. Irrigation using tube wells got a shot in the arm and Gujarat increased its cotton production to become the largest producer of cotton in the country.

The government also made a concerted effort to take electricity to every village, separating agricultural electricity from rural electricity. In one of his speeches, Modi said that to achieve better agricultural output and provide electricity to rural areas was a big challenge because '*hamare samne hai Pakistan aur ek taraf hai registan*' (we have Pakistan in front and the desert on one side). In the 2012 Gujarat assembly elections, Modi again won in his constituency by 86,373 votes and BJP won 115 of the 182 seats, a clear majority. Modi became CM for the fourth consecutive time.

Arriving on the National Scene

'A little more persistence, a little more effort,
and what seemed hopeless failure may turn to glorious success.'

—Elbert Hubbard

Seen as a go-getter and a man with a 'can-do attitude', Narendra Modi played a significant role in the 2009 general elections. Though the United Progressive Alliance (UPA) formed the

Government, the BJP was the second-largest party with 159 seats. In the run-up to the general elections of 2014, Modi was appointed to the BJP Parliamentary Board, the party's highest decision-making body. He was also appointed chairperson of the BJP's Central Election Committee for the upcoming election, and soon after declared as the party's prime ministerial candidate.

A Campaign like No Other

He fought the election from two seats (Varanasi and Vadodra) and won both, defeating Aam Aadmi Party (AAP) leader Arvind Kejriwal in Varanasi and Madhusudan Mistry of the Indian National Congress (INC) in Vadodara. Modi's manifesto promised speedy decisions and the removal of bureaucratic hurdles, making India a safe investing destination.

Modi used electronic media and social media to his advantage and reached out to the entire nation using Twitter, Facebook and Google Hangouts. He extensively used British-based company Musion's hologram technology, to simulatenously transmit live speeches made by him from a studio on to screens in specially equipped trucks, to reach out to millions across different venues in less than sixty days. His hi-tech campaign enabled him to address 700 such 'virtual' rallies. Besides these, he addressed more than 450 rallies personally travelling across the country.

With his charismatic oratory, he promised hope to the Indian people who had become disillusioned under the UPA's ten-year rule. People often asked, 'Can anyone change India? Can the government become proactive and progressive?' Modi responded that with the same offices, the same files and the same bureaucracy, the government could perform brilliantly and work for the people effectively. He promised better days and 'minimum government with maximum governance'—a government that would be pro-industry, pro-the common man and pro-farmers. Through his electrifying speeches he demonstrated his unconventional thinking and approach to problem-solving and kindled hope in the hearts of millions of Indians.

He once recalled someone asking him, 'What, according to you, are the two biggest challenges faced by India?' His response was, 'How to utilize the vast national resources of the country, and secondly, how to use and gainfully employ such a large young population of India.' He won millions of hearts when he said, '*Main pradhan mantri nahi, pradhan sevak ke roop mein hoon*' (I'm not a prime minister but here in the form of the prime servant to the people).

The Road Ahead

Narendra Modi was sworn in as the fifteenth prime minister of India on 26 May 2014, along with forty-five other ministers in his government. The BJP had won 282 seats and a total of 336, with their allies giving the party a massive mandate to rule the country.

In a brilliant and bold first, the prime minister invited the heads of all SAARC (South Asian Association for Regional Cooperation) countries to his swearing-in ceremony. It was the first time that a prime minister of Pakistan had attended the swearing-in of an Indian prime minister. Some of the important people attending this grand event were Pakistan PM Nawaz Sharif, Sri Lankan President Mahinda Rajapaksa and President Hamid Karzai of Afghanistan. Modi catapulted the swearing-in ceremony into a major diplomatic event.

On his very first day in his office he met these leaders and made it look like a mini-SAARC meeting—by no means a small achievement. On the same day he held his first Cabinet meeting and instructed the Special Investigation Team (SIT), comprising top bosses of the nation's premier investigative and intelligence agencies, to unearth the black money in foreign accounts. Within two days he set his agenda clearly in front of his Cabinet, laying stress on education, skill development, a strong bureaucracy, transparency, infrastructure development and stability and sustainability of government policy. Within the first four days, the prime minister of Japan rang to invite him to Japan, while the Chinese premier called him up to assure him of a robust and fruitful relationship with India.

As if a man in a hurry to get things done, Modi ordered his ministers to prepare a road map for their respective ministries and to hasten decision-making. He scrapped the group of ministers (GoM) to restore supremacy of the Prime Minister's Office (PMO) and the Cabinet. To restore confidence in the bureaucracy, he addressed all the secretaries to the government of India, assuring them of his full support, and urged them to make the decision-making process faster and more effective.

In his first address to the Sixteenth Lok Sabha on 4 June, he said, 'People of India have voted in unprecedented numbers and gave us a mandate to govern, I assure the people of the country that in this temple of democracy, every effort will be made to meet the hopes and aspirations of a common man.'

He also said that it was natural for people sitting in the Lok Sabha to feel that if things had not been done till now then how could they be done now? He reiterated the power of Indian democracy by pointing out that the number of people voting in India was greater than the number of voters in all the Western democracies put together. He emphasized that it was time to demonstrate to the world that India was a great nation and that we needed to break the shackles of being subservient in our thinking.

Leadership has a great deal to do with symbolization; it has to do with hope, aspiration, goal-setting and action. It's all about motivation and changing the mindset of people. Modi, through his interactions and speeches, clearly demonstrated all the traits of leadership.

Narendra Modi was voted to power by the people of India in the hope that he would bring change and build confidence in the system of governance, which had been shattered by the previous government, especially in its last decade of rule.

The prime minister has a huge challenge in front of him. To rule a country of 125 crore people, which has so many complex problems, internal as well as external, is no mean task. He has set himself this task and is ready to give every minute and every ounce of his energy to build a strong and prosperous India.

'Hope is being able to see that there is light despite all of the darkness.'

—Archbishop Desmond Tutu

1

SINCERITY OF PURPOSE AND FOCUSED APPROACH

Floating like a Butterfly, Stinging like a Bee

'When you get into a tight place and everything goes against you, until it seems that you cannot hold on a minute longer, never give up then, for that is just the place and time that the tide will turn.'

—Harriet Beecher Stowe

Narendra Modi brought a whiff of fresh air to the Prime Minister's Office (PMO) that had been perceived as defunct and indecisive for at least a decade. He launched his innings by setting a punishing pace for himself as well as his team, clearly demonstrating his intention to deliver on all the promises that were made by the BJP during the elections.

To first set his own house in order—the ministers and the bureaucrats—Modi started a 'discipline drive' beginning with punctuality. A biometric attendance system (BAS) was installed in all central government offices to record and monitor the entry and exit time of government officials. Modi, who himself reaches office by 9.00 a.m., expects everybody to be punctual, not only to reach office on time but also to clear files speedily and take quick decisions. He has also directed that offices and buildings be kept clean and indicated that those ministers and senior bureaucrats who are unwilling to work harder may resign. His message is on the lines of corporate work ethics, 'Perform or Perish'. At the same time, he has also told the bureaucrats to work without fear or favour and even asked them to approach him directly in case they ever face a problem.

Challenges

Managing such a diverse and highly populated country has its own challenges. Economy, international relations, skills and education, poverty, agriculture, defence, environment, energy, internal security, infrastructure and health are some of the key issues that need to be handled simultaneously. However, the biggest challenge the prime minister (PM) is facing is changing the mindset and attitude of the Indian people. A leader can set a pace, set an agenda and show a clear-cut direction, but ultimately the work has to be done by the people and by the government machinery.

Charting the course of a nation—incidentally the world's largest democracy and one that has been plagued with problems in the past—and steering it into safe waters is akin to steering a large ship, and not a small speedboat that can be turned from its path easily and quickly. To implement changes and demonstrate results will therefore take time. The nation, having suffered policy paralysis, rampant corruption and a demoralized populace for decades, will take a while to set itself firmly on a new course. Nevertheless, even if the PM has to address multiple problems simultaneously, he has to make a priority list.

Prioritizing Tasks: Local, Regional and Global

Narendra Modi's list of top national priorities includes restoring the people's confidence in the bureaucracy and asking his team for innovative ideas to bring about change in education, water, energy and building roads.

Other important areas spelt out by him are transparency, the economy (including investment reforms) and time-bound policy reforms to ensure sustainable policies. Having set the ball rolling for his ministers, the PM himself prioritized a dual target first: (i) tackling foreign policy and the building of strong relations with all those countries that matter the most to our national interest and, (ii) simultaneously setting out to notch up national self-esteem. To this end he has interacted with heads of nations and also instilled great confidence in Indians settled abroad by addressing them at every available opportunity.

Within a year of coming into power Modi has visited more than eighteen nations, interacting with heads of government and Indian diaspora. His speeches and interactions have given confidence to foreign investors, and a number of treaties have been signed during these visits. As compared to 2014, foreign direct investment (FDI) shot up several times over 2015. Opinion polls have indicated that 66 to 77 per cent Indians give Modi the thumbs up with regard to helping India attain its fullest potential.

Change in Focus

Agriculture adds only 14 to 18 per cent to the national gross domestic product (GDP), with more than 60 per cent of the population still trying to make a living from agriculture. Secondly, despite India's vast wealth of raw materials, the nation still continues, after seven decades of Independence, to export raw materials rather than finished goods.

Modi's philosophy as PM focuses on industrialization, thereby creating jobs, which will bring prosperity and augment buying power, which in turn will push the economy forward. Industrialization will also ensure that our vast national resources and young population are fully engaged. The thousands who have had to move out of the agriculture sector due to lack of income can also be absorbed by industry.

People, their expectations, undoubtedly raised by Narendra Modi in the run-up to the elections, hope for a lot from him, and quickly. Yet, they have realized that he has set the ball rolling in the right direction and that results will follow.

Need for Accountability

Modi means business. He himself is a workaholic who puts in a sixteen- to eighteen-hour work day. In the corporate world CEOs may take a break, organizations shut on Saturdays and Sundays, but a country never sleeps! That is the way Modi perceives his job, the seriousness of it, and expects his ministers and bureaucrats to keep pace with him. He has said on several occasions, 'I have till now not even taken one day off.'

Here he displays another great trait of a good leader—sustaining a working style and displaying the ability to follow up. The average leader issues directions and orders, and thereafter expects things to be done automatically. In contrast, a great leader, with a huge task in front of him, not only sets the pace, but keeps chasing targets, and keeps up the frantic pace all along.

Follow-up action is very important for Modi. If a meeting

does not conclude with 'all scores settled', another is held very soon to bring the agenda to a final closure; unfortunately, many political leaders don't have this kind of drive and determination. His ministers and senior bureaucrats have been clearly instructed to come prepared for meetings, to prepare bullet points and render crisp and clear presentations, devoid of theory or rhetoric. He wants specific action points instead of general vague theories.

As mentioned above, ministers and staff start the day at 9.00 a.m. and meetings begin at 9.30 sharp, going on, in many cases, up to lunchtime. The PM, however, continues to hold meetings till late evening.

The environment at these meetings is akin to the board meeting of a large private sector company. Most ministers leave office only after 9.00 p.m., often carrying work home with them. Staff and bureaucrats cannot leave until their ministers go home for the day. Whenever there is additional load, which happens often, the ministers call their officers early in the morning or late in the evening to get inputs and discuss pending issues.

India has not seen such an efficient and businesslike work culture in government departments for a very long time. If you can't turn the clock back, you need to press the fast forward button at once, which is precisely what Modi has done. A country which has problems on almost every front needs a government which not only works, but works fast.

Maintaining Integrity

People look upon Modi as an entrepreneurial PM who wants to set up systems that monitor productivity and accountability. Modi wants his ministers and officers to show no favours, no inefficiency and have no personal agendas in office. He has made it clear to his ministers, 'Do not employ any of your relatives as your personal secretaries.'

Being tech-savvy, Modi has sought to bring in technology-based systems to eradicate corruption. One initiative has been to link LPG (liquid petroleum gas) subsidy (a subsidy on twelve 14.2 kg cooking gas cylinders in a year) with the consumer's bank account under the Direct Benefit Transfer Scheme. The difference between the subsidized price and market price is transferred to the bank account of a consumer as soon as he books his cylinder. Thus, the benefit meant for genuine domestic consumers will reach them directly and cannot be diverted to anyone else. The scheme also ensures that the subsidy goes to only domestic users and for limited number of cylinders, saving government thousands of crores.

Turnaround Strategy and Leadership Style

*'Do what you think is right.
Don't let people make the decision of right or wrong for you.'*
—Steve Maraboli

To get a grip on all the myriad issues faced by a nation that has had several decades of bad governance is not an easy task—Modi has inherited a sluggish economy, high inflation, a corruption-ridden system and declining employment. His critics say, 'It is one thing to govern Gujarat and quite another to govern a country.' Despite being a first-timer at the job and never having worked in the centre before, Modi is expected to tame inflation, generate jobs and cut red tape to encourage private and foreign investment.

There are two styles of leadership that work best in such a situation. The first is the autocratic style—where the leader tries to push and bulldoze every policy and installs a mechanism with centralized control, demonstrating a tough, no-nonsense stance, and is prepared to use the rod wherever required.

The other style is leading from the front—it requires a firm grip on the job and needs guts. Such a leader is ready to push himself or herself into the midst of every situation, much like a commander leading men into battle by first himself walking through the minefield. This has a positive impact on the team and is very rewarding. Such leaders are omnipotent and omnipresent, but the style is difficult, highly motivating and very demonstrative.

Narendra Modi has wisely mixed these two styles and has put them to use very effectively. He has opted for centralized control to get a firm grip on the situation, and also to learn the ropes quickly—the biggest by-product of centralized control is quick learning, especially for the leader who has taken over a new organization. It gives the leader a chance to familiarize himself first-hand with every major aspect within his area of control.

Modi has used the PMO to tighten the reins and get hold of all ministries, make them accountable and perform at a pace he has set for achieving his goals. He has also had to connect with chief ministers (CMs) of states, because they play a very important part in the development process. Obviously, such a move would centralize control and to an extent even create bottlenecks in some cases.

Those who accuse him of too much of centralization had only a year before criticized the previous PM, Dr Manmohan

Singh, of having no control. One has to allow a leader to choose his style as long as results are delivered.

Today, our country needs a firm hand, a person who can push things, shake up the people and the government machinery out of its slumber and lethargy. How else can you change a system which refuses to budge? I feel there is no other better way of getting hold of things than the ways and means adopted by Narendra Modi.

Major Achievements

Besides building good relations with neighbouring countries and several Western nations, the Modi government has launched several initiatives for the common man. These initiatives—some of which are mentioned below—cut across the length and breadth of the country and will take a reasonable amount of time to be fully implemented.

1. Mudra Bank launched to assist six crore small vendors.
2. Pradhan Mantri Krishi Sinchai Yojna to ensure water supply to farmers.
3. Initiative to provide toilets in all schools.
4. More than sixteen crore bank accounts opened under Jan Dhan scheme.
5. More than three lakh crore rupees generated through coal auctions.

The PM is working on several initiatives simultaneously. Some strategies give instant results while many focus on mid- and long-term results.

The biggest challenge for the PM is how to ensure that the MPs, MLAs and corporators at the grass-roots level do not indulge in corruption and are in sync with his pace as well as his vision. A system and people who are not used to working, who have a deep-rooted 'anything goes' attitude and are ready to give or accept bribes at the drop of a hat will be difficult to mould.

Instead of expecting the PM to fix everything, people first need to fix their own mindset, their own attitude and set their own house in order.

'You can't depend on your eyes when your imagination is out of focus.'
—Mark Twain

LESSONS FROM A BRILLIANT LEADER AND SPEAKER

- **A great leader always walks the talk:** It is easy to deliver speeches but it is very difficult to deliver results. In this chapter we have examined the leadership style of Narendra Modi, which matches up with the promises that he made to the nation. He promised good, effective and transparent governance and his work philosophy tells us that he is on the right track and means business. A leader not only has to convey his vision to the masses but also has to clearly communicate the rules of the game to his entire team for implementing his vision. Modi has just done that. There are several lessons to learn from Modi's mantras for managing his mission.
- **Perform or perish:** He has very clearly communicated to his team of ministers and bureaucrats that the system must become efficient and responsive immediately.
- **An agenda with well-defined priorities:** Narendra Modi has accorded top priority to putting his government on fast-track mode. Having set the pace, he has gone full steam ahead to build a relationship with all the nations that matter.
- **Focused approach—the key to progress:** Instead of taking an easier populistic approach of giving freebies, he has taken the difficult path of making deep policy changes, which will lay a strong foundation on which a progressive India can be built.
- **Leading by example boosts the morale of a team:** Modi demonstrated his sincerity of purpose by setting a personal example. To his subordinates he comes across as punctual, to the point, and a

no-nonsense, clearly attentive and hardworking leader.
- **Integrity, accountability and transparency—the hallmarks of leadership:** Modi has communicated to the top brass that he expects them to demonstrate integrity and be fully accountable and transparent in their day-to-day work.
- **A unique leadership style:** Most political leaders focus on what they will do when they come to power, but very few have the ability to clearly spell out how they will do it. Modi, in all his speeches at home or abroad, has spelt out his philosophy and roadmap very clearly and is demonstrating it in his actions on a day-to-day basis.

2

A SPARTAN SOLDIER

Self-discipline, Spirituality and Simplicity

'Possessions, outward success, publicity, luxury—to me these have always been contemptible. I believe that a simple and unassuming manner of life is best for everyone, best for both the body and the mind.'

—Albert Einstein

A Simple and Disciplined Lifestyle

Modi's training with the RSS from the age of eight made him disciplined and organized, and it is to this that he owes his patriotism and ability and inclination to work hard. On the home front the family motto went along the lines of 'Simple living and high thinking'.

Being made the CM of Gujarat in October 2001 was his first heavyweight political appointment. And, despite achieving this title four times in a row, he lived in absolute simplicity. Smita Prakash, editor, Asian News International, while interviewing him as the CM and the BJP's prime ministerial candidate, found him to be very unassuming and leading a simple life.

She was surprised to find the spick and span sitting room utterly spartan, and devoid of any expensive showpieces. There were two ordinary chairs, a statue of Vivekananda and a few potted plants. Prakash, who had also interviewed many other powerful politicians, observed that most residences boasted expensive flooring and décor. She also observed that when Modi came into the room, he had no 'chamchas' or hangers-on, no assistants, and nobody was holding the door for him; neither did he place any preconditions for the interview. Despite his hectic campaign schedule he gave a seventy-minute interview—in contrast to most politicians in power who would claim to be very busy and give less than the desired time to the interviewer. At the end of the interview she wrote, 'In my mind I am thinking if he becomes Prime Minister, this man is going to turn 7 Race Course Road (the PM's official residence) into a monastery at this rate!'[1]

Even as PM, Modi does not expect anyone to fuss around him or touch his feet. His official banquets hosted for foreign dignitaries have menus that offer a substantial number of vegetarian dishes, while on official visits it is ensured that pure vegetarian fare is laid out for him. Even aboard his official aircraft no wine, liquor or non-vegetarian food is served. The Chinese laid out an absolutely vegetarian menu at the banquet hosted for Modi by President Xi Jinping when he visited China in May 2015. During Modi's visit to the US, when he was invited by President Barack Obama for dinner at the White House, he maintained his Navratri fast and abstained from eating.

---

[1] The full interview may be accessed at http://www.rediff.com/news/special/ls-election-smita-prakash-meeting-modi-spartan-surroundings-no-fuss-all-business/20140421.htm

For the first time an Indian PM is telling the world what he wants, and the world is responding well. Wearing khadi and a Gandhi cap is one thing, but making and following your own rules fastidiously as per tradition is another. This also raises his esteem in the eyes of the world, especially the Indian community living abroad.

Early to Rise

Narendra Modi, at sixty-five, is one of the older members of his Cabinet. He sleeps only five hours a night, and irrespective of the time he goes to sleep, is up by 5.00 a.m. every day. He starts his day with a cup of tea and then does yoga and pranayam.

He has a very light breakfast and fruits before he starts his first official assignment at 9.00 a.m. Before starting work he quickly goes through the PMO website, reviews certain issues and scrolls through the previous day's tweets.

He is very particular about keeping himself updated regarding national and international affairs. He therefore quickly scans through papers and the official press clippings put up to him in the morning. At night he surfs news channels during dinner, and also watches TV 'studio debates' whenever he can find the time.

He is known as a man who drives a very hard bargain and doesn't want to waste even a penny by paying more than what is required. He was renowned as having driven a hard bargain with contractors hired to execute projects in Gujarat when he was CM.

Spic and Span

Modi is a cleanliness freak. He wants his home, office and surroundings absolutely spic and span. He expects his staff to keep his surroundings clean and also does many things himself. He likes to keep his wardrobe well-organized and keeps his office desk absolutely neat and tidy.

During his younger days, he used to employ a very unique way to iron his clothes. Because electricity was not available he would take a small brass pot full of hot water and use that as an iron.

Loves Music, Books and Animals

Modi has music and rhythm in his blood. While on a state visit to Japan he played a Taiko drum solo in an impromptu jam session at the inauguration of the Technology and Culture Academy in Tokyo. During his visit to Mongolia, while meeting President Tsakhiagiin Elbegdorj he played a Mongolian musical instrument. Later in the day he tried his hand on a Yoochin, an instrument played by hitting the strings with two tiny mallets.

Modi also likes animals and makes every effort to protect and take care of them. As the CM of Gujarat he put in sustained efforts to provide quality healthcare facilities for animals and the government began regularly organizing animal husbandry fairs. Medical care, such as dental and orthopaedic treatment, is provided to the animals on such occasions. He also came up with the idea of animal hostels. More than 1,100 cows are sheltered in an animal hostel in Akarda village, a pilot project started by Modi. As a result there is no cow dung on the streets and the centrally collected cow dung is used for biogas.

As PM he doesn't get much time to read books, but since he loved reading books from his childhood he does order a few on subjects of interest and carries them with him to read while travelling by air.

A Spiritual Man

Narendra Modi is a deeply spiritual and religious person. While religion generally includes the idea of a single super being, an entity that has created the universe and which controls our destiny, the idea of spirituality is a little more porous and flexible. Spirituality is an internal process that seeks wholeness, genuineness and personal authenticity. It also takes an individual towards deriving a meaning and purpose in life. It means connecting with the self and the community. In that sense Modi is more spiritual than religious. He is a karma yogi who believes in the collective good, who loves his country, his people, and has a strong sense of purpose in life.

He connects religion and spirituality beautifully. For instance, he observes a nine-day fast during Navaratri twice a year. He looks at it as an act of self-purification. It gives him strength, resilience and makes his willpower strong. For nine days he is on a diet of fruits and lime water. He has been keeping this fast for over forty years and follows it strictly. Even if he receives an invitation to dinner at the White House, or has to attend a meeting with American CEOs, he observes this fast strictly and without fail and goes on with his speeches, official meetings and every other official engagement as per schedule. There's no cutting back on his programme.

Modi truly believes that the country will progress only when our countrymen practice the principles given in the ancient scriptures of India. He connects with religious leaders like Sri Sri Ravi Shankar, Mata Amritanandamayi and other spiritual leaders very well. He has a strong belief that India will become a world leader in the near future and, according to him, one of the reasons is our strong spiritual and traditional values.

Modi and Yoga

Narendra Modi practises yoga almost 300 days in a year. It is not how much you do, but how regular you are that matters. He combines yoga, pranayam and meditation.

In the last fifteen years, TV has made yoga very visible. People like Baba Ramdev have contributed immensely to its popularity and have exploited the electronic media positively to reach out to millions of Indians, both in India and abroad. Yoga is perceived by all as something entirely Indian, and is one thing which every Indian is proud of.

While addressing the United Nations (UN) General Assembly Modi urged world leaders to realize the benefits of yoga and to start a World Yoga Day. His appeal convinced the Assembly and, in a proud moment for India, the UN adopted 21 June as 'International Day of Yoga'. International Yoga Day will always be seen as his brainchild.

In all, 177 nations supported Narendra Modi's proposal when he said,

> We need to change our lifestyle. For us in India, respect for nature is an integral part of spiritualism. We treat nation's bounties as sacred. Yoga is an invaluable gift of our ancient tradition. Yoga embodies unity of mind and body, thought and action, restrained fulfilment, harmony between man and nature, a holistic approach to health and well-being. It is not about exercise, but to discover the sense of oneness with yourself, the world and the nature... Let us work towards adopting an International Yoga Day.

'Simplify your life. You don't grow spiritual, you shrink spiritual.'
—Steve Maraboli

LESSONS FROM A BRILLIANT LEADER AND SPEAKER

- **Simple lifestyle:** Many great leaders leave an indelible impact on people because of a simple lifestyle. Modi, though fond of dressing well, comes across as a man who believes in frugal living.
- **Being spiritual and God-fearing:** Men and women who are spiritual and God-fearing can leave an imperishable impact on their audience. Narendra Modi is not only disciplined in his work and life, but is also disciplined in practising spirituality. He religiously fasts and yet goes about his daily official chores without a pause.
- **Being proud of one's heritage and culture:** When Modi tells Indians to be proud of their heritage and culture, he appears to be very authentic, because he himself follows Indian traditions fastidiously.
- **Cultivating the fine arts and a reading habit add to one's personality:** Narendra Modi loves music. He sometimes plays musical instruments for fun and relaxation and is fond of reading. His reading habits help him build content and knowledge and his music keeps him warm and energetic.
- **Effective managers and leaders are pretty well organized:** They never appear dishevelled and are always well-dressed. Narendra Modi is always immaculately dressed for the occasion and looks fresh and relaxed when he stands on the dais to speak to his audience.
- **Remaining fit and healthy is important for everyone:** One has to spare a reasonable amount of time to exercise. Being regular with exercise is

the mantra for staying fit. Despite a hectic schedule, the PM takes time out for his daily dose of yoga and pranayam.
- **A good speaker must remain abreast of current affairs:** Reading newspapers or listening to the news on TV or the radio is essential. Modi makes efforts to remain updated by watching TV and reading newspapers as much as time permits.

3

DIFFERENT AUDIENCE, DIFFERENT STROKES

Speaking from the Heart

'There is nothing in the world like a persuasive speech to fuddle the mental apparatus and upset the convictions and debauch the emotions of an audience not practised in the tricks and delusions of oratory.'

—Mark Twain

Who is your audience; who are you speaking to? This is one of the most important aspects of oratory. Your audience matters and therefore you need to tailor your script according to this fundamental tenet of 'context'. The speaker must also keep in mind the mood of the time, the public sentiment and thereby understand and gauge the expectations of the audience. In short, you should know what the audience wants to hear. A good orator is in absolute sync with the tide of public emotions. And that is how he can speak from his heart to reach out to their hearts. If you are speaking to CEOs and senior executives at a business summit, for instance, you need to rise up to their expectations in terms of content, examples, relevance and facts.

You need to fulfil their aspirations such that they have some effective takeaway from what you say. You also need to understand the prevalent environment and the end result that you want to achieve. If you are addressing a business summit during recession, your tone, your examples, your approach will be entirely different from when you address the same audience during a victory celebration or an economic turnaround. A great orator recognizes problems, remembers details, responds to situations and reiterates important issues, keeping in mind the level of the audience and the prevailing circumstances.

Addressing a science conference or a technology summit will require two entirely different approaches. The audience has the same maturity level but the contexts are different. Yet again the entire approach will change when you address college students and will further dramatically change when speaking to schoolchildren. Stories, examples and explanations have to be much simpler in the latter case. Your body language, facial expressions, tone, pitch and speed of delivery would also depend on the context and your audience.

The ultimate art of oratory demands a chameleon-like approach. One should be able to transform according to the occasion, the audience, the mood and the situation. Much like an actor, who very easily and comfortably moves from one character to another, from one scripted role to another, a great orator can change colour like a chameleon, at will.

Narendra Modi—Master of the Moment

Narendra Modi has mastered the craft of reaching out to the hearts of his audience. He can mesmerize the people because he appears genuine. He can win over people because he speaks from his heart and means what he says. He knows what's in the air, what people feel, what people expect and what people want. He seems to understand their pain, their expectations and their aspirations. This doesn't come easy. These are the things which are neither taught in business schools nor in coaching classes; these need to be learnt in self-study mode, and in a continuous manner over a period of time. Armed with this understanding Modi invents his speech, as if instantaneously.

He tailors his speech to the audience, and it fits them to a T. Hope is never a matter of the head; it is a matter of the heart. Modi has learnt how to win hearts. His outstanding communication skills have been a major contributor to his political ascent, his ability to motivate the nation and positioning India as a force to reckon with in the international arena. No wonder everyone from schoolchildren to CEOs and the common man describe him as powerful, mesmerizing and charismatic. His style is compelling and eloquent.

He has mastered the art of conveying his vision, expressing his ambitions, instilling confidence and motivating his audience—taking them to a different high every time he speaks.

During his election campaign for the nation's top post, he combined his style with substance, his charisma with character and his enthusiasm with energy. He galvanized and roused the young, the middle-aged and the old to come and vote for change, a meaningful change towards progress and prosperity for all. He effectively connected with people of all religions, people from different regions speaking different languages and belonging to diverse and disparate segments of society.

He cleverly and intelligently transformed an election campaign into a national movement, a Jan Andolan or people's movement—a movement towards development and prosperity for all—'*Sabka saath, sabka vikas*' (If everyone's together, everyone will progress).

Stage Presence

After being elected and sworn in as the prime minister of the world's largest democracy, Modi did not stop his motivational campaign. In fact, he stepped it up. That is what India needed, what Indians needed for their sagging morale, for their feeling of hopelessness and despair. In many of his speeches, he said, 'Most of you feel nothing can be done. Many of you feel we were unlucky to be born in India. That is why many of you want to leave the country and settle abroad. Don't worry, things will change. *Ab acche din ayenge* (Now good days will come).'

He gave hope to one and all. It was an oft-heard comment: 'We feel proud that we have a PM who speaks like a PM and behaves like a PM.' Many said, 'Here is the man who will do something big, he will turn India around.' Modi was thus undoubtedly acknowledged as an outstanding speaker, a man of a never-seen-before calibre on the Indian political arena.

Narendra Modi speaks clearly, emphatically and with full confidence. He has the ability to control his voice, his pitch and pauses, so as to deliver a resounding performance. He can alter the texture of his voice, change his facial expressions to reflect extreme seriousness or suddenly smile after delivering a pun.

He usually holds the lectern with both hands, demonstrating that he is in full control. He looks from left to right, gazing at his audience from one side to the other. His gaze is captivating and reassuring. He appears very confident and keeps his composure even if someone interrupts, especially during parliamentary debates and discourses.

Modi uses his hands, arms and fingers intelligently. To emphasize a point as gospel truth, he raises the index finger of his right hand (sometimes his left) in the air for a while, usually till he completes his point.

He also makes a gesture of sincerity and honesty by making a circle with his index finger and his thumb. This also indicates finality of a statement, its perfection and its genuineness. To show solidarity and as a display of power he sometimes raises his fist in the air. At appropriate moments, where he needs to show strength, he holds both fists in the air.

Sometimes, to convey something very serious and intriguing, he partly opens his palm and moves it around his wrist, with an expression of astonishment on his face. When he talks of inclusive development ('sabka vikas'), he opens his arms wide with palms facing upwards, as though welcoming everyone. In a rare gesture, he thumps his chest—'chhati thokke'—to assert his achievements or demonstrate his resolve. With these gestures, he brings himself closer to the audience and his discourse doesn't remain a public discourse, but becomes a one-to-one connect with each person in the audience.

The most important observation here is that to his audience, it doesn't appear rehearsed. These gestures can't be rehearsed because every occasion, every dialogue is different and one has to master the craft of using one's hands and gestures to connect with the context and content. There is a sense of expectation, a sense of anticipation, a sense of 'What's coming next?' from his audience every time he stands up to speak.

Modi appears to speak extempore. This is definitely a gift of God. Yet, one can achieve such a spectacular performance again and again with practice. He is like a trained pilot—the more you fly, the better you become. Your take-offs and landings become smoother, flying becomes effortless and you can handle rough weather anytime during the flight with ease. And, as a Top Gun, you are great at aerobatics, manoeuvring and gliding through the skies comfortably.

Modi seldom falters, rarely fumbles and is never short of appropriate words or phraseology. His flow is perfect, delivery flawless and each of his ideas is beautifully strung to the next, as if by a craftsman assembling a necklace of pearls.

This is ultimate mastery of oratory. Modi excels at touching the hearts and souls of children, the youth, veterans, scientists, soldiers, the high and mighty and even the masses.

After assuming charge as PM, Modi has addressed millions of people at home as well as abroad. He has addressed the Indian Parliament, spoken at the Civil Services Day, 21 April 2015, addressing senior bureaucrats, addressed children across the country on Teacher's Day and addressed the Indian diaspora in the US, Canada, China, France, Australia and several other countries with equal eloquence and ease. He has shown the same competence whether addressing the BJP MP's workshop or the Rajya Sabha or a political rally or the US's Council on Foreign Relations.

His approach has uniformly been focused, his content tailormade and his style measured to suit the occasion. Speaking at United Nations Educational, Scientific and Cultural Organization (UNESCO), addressing students of Delhi University or Tsinghua (a university in Beijing) or Fudan University in Shanghai, he has held audiences in awe. For the elite and the intellectual, his motivational speech at the Indian Space Research Organization (ISRO), his vision- and mission-oriented speech at the Economics Times Summit for Indian corporate head honchos, and his address at the Indian Science Congress have all been masterpieces in themselves. Let us now analyse some of these speeches.

First Lok Sabha Address

In his first address to the Lok Sabha, Modi demonstrated humility by saying, 'This is my first opportunity to speak to such an august audience, with many in the house having an experience of thirty to forty years. *Paramparayen bahut unchi hain* (The values and traditions are very high). If I make a mistake, please forgive me as I am new.'

The opposition made some noise at this point, but Modi kept his cool and proceeded unperturbed. He paid respect to all the earlier speakers and acknowledged their greatness. He then moved on to set the pace, 'All of you are saying how will you do all that you have said and promised to the countrymen. *Aisa sochna bahut swabhawik hai* (It is natural to think this way).'

To substantiate his point, he narrated an incident from when he was the chief minister of Gujarat:

> In [the] Gujarat Assembly on the very first day I said I will provide 24/7 electricity to all villages. People in the Assembly could not believe this… One very senior member from the opposition came and met me after the session and said, *'Modiji, aapse koi chook to nahin ho gai?'* (I hope you have not made a mistake here?) As the state was short of 2,000 megawatts of energy, he wanted to know how will I do it? He asked with a genuine concern, but we did it… We will make all efforts to achieve what we have said…

He added that he was a hopeful candidate prior to being elected, but was now the protector of the people's hopes. He noted that it was an auspicious omen that 125 crore people had voted for him and the party.

This was a great start, which set the pace for the rest of the speech. This was finely calibrated political rhetoric.

> Have we projected ourselves as a great democracy? We have more people voting than voters in the US and Europe put together... *Hum do sau saal ki gulami ke baad kabhi kabhi bade aadmi ke aagey bol nahin sakte. Kabhi kabhi toh chamri ka rang bhi asar kar jata hai* (After 200 years of foreign rule, we sometimes do not have the guts to speak in front of someone powerful. Sometimes it is also due to the colour of their skin. The time has come that we must project ourselves as a great people and great democracy.)

And with this remark he put the entire opposition on the backfoot, because he was stating a fact.

Modi has a great gift of coming up with out-of-the-box ideas. His vision and mission are crystal clear. He also moves from macro to micro issues with ease, and gives a reason for everything he says. Defining his vision for rural India, he demanded broadband connectivity in every village. He envisioned distance education through satellite. He once said, '*Har jawan ladka apne gaon mein rehna chahta hai* (Every village boy wants to stay at home in his village and with his parents). But he doesn't have a means of livelihood. Can we not provide him with agro-based industry in his village itself?'

He added that we need to change our attitude and become more efficient, citing an example, 'If a railway godown has tomatoes and marble to be transported, the railway clerk will load the marble first and tomatoes later. Does he not understand that the tomatoes will rot and he should dispatch them first?'

These are small things, but Modi demonstrates his understanding of the problems on ground. His speech emphasized the need for real-time data on agro-products so that the rural poor could earn a living. He then immediately shifted to a macro level by saying, 'Sikkim is doing a great job and is becoming an organic state. Can't we make it a great exporter of organic items for which there is a demand across the world? The central government will help Sikkim achieve this.'

He further dwelt on agriculture and expected agricultural universities to do research for more production per hectare—'More crop per drop'. He explained that pulses were the only means for a poor person to get proteins. 'We need research to produce better and cheaper pulses. We can tackle malnutrition only with pulses. We also need to modernize the Food Corporation of India (FCI); while we produce more we need to distribute it effectively.' He finished this point using great rhetoric, 'If we don't do this, our soul will not forgive us.'

Question-and-answer Session with Schoolchildren on Teacher's Day

On this occasion Narendra Modi answered questions posed by schoolchildren. He smiled and looked relaxed so that the children would be comfortable. Given below are excerpts from this exchange.

Question: How did good education and good teachers influence your life?

Answer: Let me explain with an example. If you haven't got the right education, you will not be able to correctly learn from experiences. If someone picks your pocket and if you haven't got the right education, you will become a pickpocket yourself. But if your education is good, you will learn to keep your money safely. Therefore teachers and education have mattered in my life.

Question: Did you ever think that you would become the Prime Minister one day?

Answer: I am from a very ordinary background. I never even became a class monitor in school. If you have big expectations and you are unable to achieve them, you get disappointed. You want to become a doctor or an engineer and you can't become one, you will regret it all your life. Whatever you are enjoy that. *Karne ke sapne dekho, banne ke nahi*. (Dream of doing something rather than becoming someone.)

Question: Can you share some of your pranks at school?

Answer: I will tell you, if you promise that you will not do this. Masti (fun) is an important part of life. Every child does masti. During a function when there was a music programme and musicians were playing 'shehnai' (flute) we used to take 'imli' (tamarind) and dangle it in front of the musicians; their mouths used to water and they could not play! I will now tell you something very naughty. But you don't do it. Promise you will not do it? During wedding functions we used to staple together clothes of ladies and gents from behind. You can imagine what chaos would ensue thereafter.

Question: How can we schoolchildren contribute to the nation?

Answer: Cleanliness is important. After school hours when you reach home, keep your schoolbags, your shoes and clothes at the right place. Ask your mother how much the monthly electricity bill is. Find ways of reducing that amount. If it is Rs 400, can we make it Rs 300? What needs to be done—discuss with your parents. Remember, what you save will go to the poor. Do tree plantation. You don't have to do big things to serve your country.

Question: How can we save energy?

Answer: Sleep with your windows open so that you don't require an air conditioner, or even a fan. It is cheaper to save electricity than to produce it. When you brush teeth don't let the tap remain on. You will save water. These small things are very important. *Boond boond se sagar bharta hai* (Small drops make up an ocean).

Question: Are you like a headmaster?

Answer: Your headmaster is here? He will get very annoyed with this *(smiling)*. Yes I am a hard taskmaster. But I myself work very hard. I told my officers [that] if you work for eleven hours, I will work for twelve and if you work for twelve, I will work for thirteen hours.

The above interaction demonstrates his ability to understand the level of his audience and accordingly fine-tune his words to reach out to people in the most appropriate manner. He cleverly brings in humour and shares his childhood pranks to strike a connect with young schoolchildren.

Twenty-Fifth NASSCOM Foundation Day

The day after the interaction with schoolchildren, while addressing industry honchos at the Twenty-fifth NASSCOM Foundation Day, Modi easily changed gears to reach out to them at their level of understanding and talk about what mattered to them.

Modi demonstrated his clarity of vision and his firm grip on technology, especially its applications, when he addressed a gathering of technocrats. Speaking in Hindi, he managed to deliver a speech which was not only motivational but clearly and concisely laid down the roadmap for the IT industry. He made concrete suggestions and put forth his high expectations from the software industry.

He started by saying, '*Yeh ek janandolan ban gaya hai* (This has become a people's revolution).Otherwise rarely does an industry sector grow so fast.' Paying tribute to Dewang Mehta, founder of NASSCOM, he said that his efforts had created a beautiful necklace of beads. 'Twenty-five years and you have moved from a $100 million industry to $146 billion.' Displaying his ability to chip in humour, he said, 'One reason for this success is that government is not in it. The further we stay, the better it is. Lakhs have jobs, the economy has grown and the world's attitude towards us has changed. Now we want as many "i-ways" as we want highways.'

He then linked governance and technology:

> We need to do a lot for governance. Imagine 100 crore mobile users, all reachable. If you prepare mobile apps quickly it will be a great help. Hindustan is moving forward very quickly. Let me share a small incident.When I was the Chief Minister of Gujarat, I wanted to visit a backward area. So I asked my officers to organize a visit. They built a training centre at a cost of 25 lakh and I was asked to inaugurate it. When I reached there I saw more than 100 women, who had come there to sell milk, taking photographs of the centre and myself on their mobiles! I asked them what they were going

> to do with the photographs and you'll be astonished at their reply. They said, "We'll go home and download them." You can estimate that if tribal people know this much then what can we not do with technology?...
>
> I want to say something, please don't be offended. I have the greatest expectations from you. If we can go to Mars, why couldn't we create Google? We must now work on these lines. Cyber security is a great opportunity. I have met several heads of state since becoming the PM, at least thirty have expressed this need. I am talking to you as a client. If we don't provide security, a day will come when people will be scared of using the mobile. Then you will get a shock.

Displaying his typical out-of-the-box thinking he urged the software industry to work on digital databases, and added jokingly, 'You will have to lower your status to do this; we can even keep gold bonds in a cloud locker.' Throwing another challenge to them he said, '*Sarkar silos mein kaam karti hai. Har office mein data alag alag format, alag alag software par hai. Kya hum is raw data ko synchronize nahin kar saktey? Yeh governance mein bahut kaam ayega.*' (The government works in silos. Every office uses different software for their data. Can't we synchronize this raw data? It will be very useful in governance.)

Illustrating what technology can do he said,

> We took advantage of the Supreme Court ruling [on the coal scam]. We used technology to auction coal blocks...When the CAG report stated that there has been a Rs 186,000 crore fraud, nobody was willing to believe it. We also spoke politically, but did think if could actually be that much. Thanks to the technology, an auction was conducted in a transparent manner and the government has recovered [Rs] 110,000 crore until now.

Coming up with yet another out-of-the-box idea, he talked about tourism in India. 'Tourism is a three-trillion-dollar business. Can't we make fifty virtual heritage museums? What a great opportunity this is that lies in front of you.'

Moving to another area, he said, 'Long-distance education is a big challenge and opportunity. Wouldn't your 1,800 members like to give their school an e-library? You can definitely do that much for the school you studied in.'

Then talking about changing times he said,

> Earlier a nice watch and a pen were status symbols, now it's a good mobile; but an affordable mobile is good too. I had an uncle who bought a watch costing 2.5 lakh and started showing it off in front of my nephew. My nephew asked, 'What's the time on your watch?' Uncle replied, 'It's eight now.' The nephew said, 'Mine cost Rs 250 and it's eight on this one too.'

Modi comes out as a winner every time not only because of the way he speaks, but more importantly because of his clarity of thought, his simple yet practical ideas, his innovative spirit and his willingness to experiment and take risks. He speaks on topics that everyone understands, he articulates beautifully and speaks from his heart. He motivates, pushes and nudges his audience at appropriate times and for appropriate reasons. His remarks are very rarely sarcastic and never caustic. He applauded the IT industry, yet pointed out some flaws and further gave them ideas for collaborating with the government.

103rd Session of the Indian Science Congress

Modi addressed thousands of scientists acknowledging, at the outset, the contribution of science for betterment of society in fields like health, eradicating hunger, creating clean energy and giving humanity a better chance of survival. He reached out to the scientific community in the most appropriate way, appreciated their achievements and tried to understand their problems. He thus again demonstrated his ability to relate to everyone, irrespective of their field or age or level of education, be they schoolchildren or senior scientists.

'The arms of science must reach the poor by giving them cleaner cities, better environment, water management, housing and sanitation. For this, universities, national laboratories and researchers must come together and work. You need more passion than resources,' Modi said.

Modi demonstrated his understanding of science and its inherent problems by saying,

> There is an uncertainty in research, yet we need to work to find solutions in biotechnology, nanoscience and agriculture. I also want scientists working in the Central Institutes of Research to spend sometime teaching in universities, and guiding PhD students. Industry must step up investment in research. Don't work only in key areas but also try to use traditional and local knowledge for the benefit of mankind. Children must be proud of our scientists. We should have scientists as role models as muchas we do sportsmen. We must showcase our scientific achievements at the Republic Day parade. We need to celebrate scientific achievements. Let us revive the romance of science, rekindle the love of science in children. Let me assure you, you will have no better supporter than me and I have seen your support in making a great India.

He received a resounding ovation from the scientific community. In that brief half-an-hour, heart-to-heart talk, Modi showed that he considered them heroes, and that made him their hero.

Address to the Indian Railways

Modi is no doubt a great visionary and motivator. While addressing railway staff at the inauguration of a diesel locomotive workshop at Varanasi he said,

> *Main railway ko vikas ki reed ki haddi dekhna chahta hoon. Kyun na hum railway infrastructure ka poora istemal karen? Rural areas mein kai station hain jahan sirf ek ya do gaadi din mein aati hai. Aise railway station per bijli paani aur road ki suvidha hai. Kyun na hum wahan skill development classes chalayen?*
> (I want to make the railways the backbone of progress. Why don't we make full use of railway infrastructure? There are many stations in rural areas where only one or two trains arrive per day. These stations have facilities like water, electricity and roads. Why don't we start skill development classes there?)

He then threw them a challenge, '96 per cent of all components for railway bogies and engines are made in India. I want that 4 per cent also to be made in India. The railways are the greatest strength. We need infrastructure management practices, modern technology and service orientation.'

Modi has a knack of motivating, setting expectations, giving directions, suggesting solutions—all at once. This is the great ability of an orator. This comes with experience, understanding and hard work.

Strategic Intent

As prime minister of the world's largest democracy, he has a grand vision, a very clear focus and a working methodology to achieve this. He knows that it is not easy to turn around such a large, overpopulated country, where citizens speak several languages and belong to different religions.

In his first year as PM, he wanted to motivate people to

come together and help him realize his vision. He also wanted to reach out to the world through their political leadership and buy them in, because without the support of some key foreign powers it would not be possible to fulfil his dreams, the common man's dreams and, in fact, India's dreams.

At home he has therefore addressed every stakeholder, bureaucrat, the Parliament, the entire scientific community, the industry, media, economists, the judiciary, the armed forces and the entire political class.

Abroad, he has kindled a million hearts. He has spoken to the Indian diaspora wherever he has gone, raised their self-esteem and raised Indian's prestige in the eyes of other nations. He has addressed the G20 summit, spoken at UNESCO, addressed the United Nations General Assembly, shared platforms to speak along with heads of states and addressed the political community and industry czars abroad.

It requires clarity of thought, preparation, guts, knowledge and above all energy to deliver so many speeches and within such a short duration to different people, with different educational backgrounds, speaking different languages, with different understandings and from different nations.

Modi has come out a winner on the oratory platform, like no one before. A master craftsman, he transforms into a different avatar in different settings in front of different audiences. To some he is a teacher, to others a great motivator; some see him as a leader and many as a saviour. Modi has proved himself to be a master orator.

'I am a firm believer in the people. If given the truth,
they can be depended upon to meet any national crisis.
The great point is to bring them the real facts.'

—Abraham Lincoln

DIFFERENT AUDIENCE, DIFFERENT STROKES

LESSONS FROM A BRILLIANT LEADER AND SPEAKER

- To tailor your speech according to the audience is probably one of the most important facets of public speaking. A good orator will talk about the same subject and similar issues differently in front of different types of audiences. Simply put, such speakers are like chameleons that can change colour at will, depending on the environment and the background.
- Narendra Modi has mastered this art and, with his oratory, won the hearts of young and old alike, infusing a spirit of hope and enthusiasm in millions of Indians during his election campaign, which he turned into a People's Movement or Jan Andolan and made it look like a collective effort of the people and his party to usher in change.
- Modi captures the imagination of the audience each time he speaks. There is a sense of anticipation, a sense of expectation from his audience every time he stands up to speak.
- Modi's speeches don't appear to be rehearsed. They are flawless and flow extremely smoothly, with no apparent rough edges. He has a marvellous stage presence; he dominates with ease.
- One has to learn a great deal regarding body language from Narendra Modi's stage performance. He uses his hands, his fingers, his arms and his facial expression exactly as required in synchronization with his perfect dialogue delivery.
- Narendra Modi appears to be inventing as he speaks. This is the ultimate in oratory, a craft par excellence. And this he does with absolute ease

regardless of the level, the background of the audience or even the topic and occasion.
- Lawyers argue in front of judges; business executives speak in boardrooms, seminars or conferences; teachers address students; but Narendra Modi speaks to everybody; and has spoken to a variety of people in India as well as abroad. From schoolchildren to seasoned parliamentarians, from the Indian Science Congress to economic forums; and from bureaucrats to the Indians diaspora, he has been able to motivate people to rally behind him—achieving his strategic intent of selling his vision to his countrymen and the people abroad who matter.

4

FACTS AT YOUR FINGERTIPS

Develop the Art of Using Logic to Convey Your Vision

'The finest eloquence is that which gets things done.'
—David Lloyd George

There is nothing more convincing than logical reasoning and cold facts. Logic and fact, juxtaposed with emotions and rhetoric, can sway public opinion powerfully, even while dealing with the most stubborn, most learned and most informed audience.

Narendra Modi knows that people have faith in him. To keep his own hope, and people's hopes, afloat he has to not only convince the hearts but conquer the minds of people. He has to show them the real picture of where we are, where we can go, and how he is going to get us there. He has to work hard and convince people that a lot can be done. If this can be achieved, the people of India will back him to the hilt to fulfil his dreams, to fulfil India's dream.

To do these things, Modi uses logic and rattles off cold facts and figures to present his case and his vision. Alongside, he tells people what all has been done till now. He beautifully combines logic, satire, humour and an emotional approach to tell the people that he is here to stay and he is going to achieve all that he has said he will.

Modi has the skill of subtly combining facts with emotions; he can use figures to present a watertight case. Addressing the US's Council on Foreign Relations he said, in Hindi,

> People have aspirations after a long time, they saw so much negativity that now they have huge aspirations. Earlier, it was easy because politicians could handle small isolated groups and make them happy. This way, they kept vote banks intact. Today people want something new. People want progress, good governance. We are the youngest nation with the oldest civilization; stability of government is a big message. *Janata ne neev dali hai* (The people have laid the foundation). At the same time, today government administration is the biggest burden. Now the middle class has just come out of poverty and it doesn't want to go back to poverty. If we don't handle it and the middle class falls back into poverty the people will lose faith. Even if a person falls sick, he wants his own doctor, because he has faith in him and him alone. Similarly, the government must restore faith in the people.

He then moved onto specifics, 'We want to run the economy on three pillars: agriculture, 30 per cent; manufacturing, 30 per cent; and the service sector, 30 per cent, so that if one doesn't do well, the other two can support it.' He based his logic on the foundations of age-old wisdom: don't put all your eggs in one basket. He also conveyed that all sectors must get an equal chance. 'Whatever we produce should have zero defect and zero effect—zero effect meaning zero effect on the environment.'

Modi is a great teacher. He reaches out to his colleagues who are from diverse backgrounds in the most simplistic way. He urges them to act together and speak about their achievements. He explains to his party people why he is doing what he is doing, as, for example, in the speech below at a workshop for BJP MPs when he talked about the nuclear energy deficit,

> How do we go green? No one gives us nuclear technology and no one gives us nuclear fuel. This happens because the nation which wants to oblige is also under international pressure not to give. We have gone ahead and progressed in space research but we have been left behind in the nuclear race, for clean energy....We don't talk enough about our achievements. We must tell the people what we are doing, what we have done and what we want to do. We have to create that 'echo effect' to keep the trust intact.

When the opposition taunted Modi, saying he was merely renaming their policies, he retorted, 'The names are new but the problems are old. These problems are your inheritance to us. You should be happy that we are finding solutions.'

Reacting to another remark he said, 'First people would ask us where we (the BJP) were during the fight for Independence. We asked them where they were during the 1857 mutiny. We should not get caught up in such nitpicking... Governments come and go; ideology, philosophy stays.'

Talking of the schemes initiated under the Mahatma Gandhi National Rural Employee Guarantee Act (MNREGA) by the UPA Government during a Lok Sabha address he said,

> My politics state I cannot shut down MNREGA. You had dug a ditch because of MNREGA. That was your weakness and I will keep on beating the drum about this... Corruption has destroyed this country. We get caught up in whose shirt

> is whiter, we need to find solutions together... You are very experienced, you must definitely guide us... We will give a policy-driven governance. All policies may not be faultless but we will ensure minimum grey areas. We have political will and we are making efforts.

He then pointed to some stark realities and said, 'We require toilets for schools. We need 4.25 lakh toilets, 1.5 lakh to be newly constructed and the rest need repair. Complete mapping has been done. 65,000 have already been made. We need to make one toilet per second to achieve this huge target!'

Then he delivered a master blow: 'We don't trust our citizens. Why do they have to get every paper attested by some government officer? Why can't they self-attest them? My visa was rejected, I was ridiculed, I was disrespected... How many hundreds of projects are stuck—if the bridge is ready, there is no road on either side; if the roads are ready, the bridge takes years to build.'

As seen above, Modi addresses disparate points in a single speech with such ease and elan that the audience does not perceive each point as a separate thread but as a well-woven fabric with different colours and textures.

Addressing the students of Delhi University during his election campaign he noted,

> After more than six decades of Independence we are still looking for swaraj. We are looking for good governance. Today the government is firefighting. It runs to wherever there is a fire. The government needs to visualize. We have failed on this count. There is a hopeless feeling that everybody is a thief and that nothing can be done. People want to leave the country and go. My experience tells me that we can still move forward with the same laws, the same people, the same

institutions and the same files… An ambassador asked me what India's two main problems were. I said that our greatest problem was that 65 per cent of our population was under thirty-five years of age. How do we use them? Secondly, we have such rich natural resources in eastern India, how do we use them properly? We want to export finished products, not raw material.

Modi is quick to point out faults and doesn't mince words while presenting the reality. And people love it. He speaks out his vision: 'We need skills not certificates.' He quotes in this context from one of the many books written by Dr Dada Dharmadhikari, who was a companion of Vinoba Bhave, 'Somebody approached him for a job, so he asked him, "What can you do?" The man said he was a graduate. Dharmadhikari again asked, "No. What do you do?" and the man again said, "I am a graduate." He got the same answer three times. Our graduates are unemployable.' Modi reiterated elsewhere that his main concern was how to make the large under-thirty-five-years' populace skilled. 'We have to become Skill India from Scam India. We have to make a separate Ministry of Skill Development. We must have a slogan of Shram Mev Jayate.'

Speaking at the Rajya Sabha one time, he said, 'Policies cannot be based on perception today. Goa and Nagaland have Christians, J&K has Muslims, Punjab has Sikhs, and they all have BJP governments. Then how is BJP a Hindu party?' He also dismantled the opposition's charge that his government was pro-corporate.

> If we are building toilets and schools and issuing Soil Cards, what are we making for corporates? Is skill-development for the benefit of the corporates? Forty per cent of the population

is linked economically to the Ganga. Is the clean-up of the Ganga for the corporates too? Are we building small, affordable housing for the corporates? It is not so, we have to give people a livelihood, we have to lay emphasis on skill development. We want skilled hands.

Narendra Modi demonstrates an ability to identify real problems which need to be taken care of. He presents his case with facts and figures, with complete conviction. He uses common sense to seek solutions. He uses simple yet powerful expressions.

Speaking in Parliament about the safety of women, he raised the level of the discussion by several notches with one sentence, 'We should not do psychological analysis of rape. Does it bring us any honour by doing so?'

Talking about micro entrepreneurs in the Rajya Sabha he said, 'Today the common man sells fruits, milk and bread or repairs scooters to make a living. These are the men who give employment to one or two people more.' Then he added, 'There are 5.5 crore units which give eleven or twelve crore jobs. Nobody gives these people money or a loan. Their solution lies in microfinance schemes that will help the poor in building a livelihood.'

Based on this, the Micro Unit Development and Refinance Agency (MUDRA) was launched, which gives loans from Rs 50,000 to Rs 10 lakh to small entrepreneurs.

Addressing the Economics Times Global Summit, Modi said, 'We have missed chances, we have unlimited possibilities. Today we are at less than 4 per cent growth, governance is at rock bottom. We cannot afford this. We can't afford telecom scams. We have to repair the damage; you will have the full support of my government.'

Talking about the administrative system of the government, he accepted the reality as the PM and said that the government system is complex and slow.

> In Hindu mythology you get moksh [nirvana] after going to char dham [four pilgrimage-destinations]. A file in a government department goes to thirty-six dhams and still doesn't get any moksh. We need to simplify processes. I want a sharp, effective, fast and flexible system. There are areas where the private sector will do better. In fact, the government has no business to be in business.

For the nation and his government he defined his formula 'Skill, scale and speed' to compete with the rest of the world.

Modi spelt out what was required,

> A state is meant to do only five things: (i) public good such as defence, judiciary and police; (ii) environment; (iii) market control; (iv) information regarding genuineness of products; and (v) welfare for those at the lowest rungs of society in areas like education and health. The government has to see how much money it is spending and what it is getting. We are a 2 trillion economy. Can we dream of a 20 trillion economy? Should we not create a foundation by doing groundwork for that? We aim to do that and that is hard work. Improvement is a continuous process.

Referring to financial leakages he said, 'Subsidies are needed for the poor; I repeat, subsidies are needed for the poor. We need to plug leakages, and wastage must be eliminated… To make the poor fit to fight poverty we will have to think about mass production and production by the masses.'

As we can see from the above, while presenting a case it is very important to state the reality of the situation to define the existing problems, as also to spell out achievements in real time as they happen. An orator must enumerate achievements. Communicating is not only a means of branding but also an opportunity for reassuring the audience.

Narendra Modi is not only a thinker but a doer. He pushes his agenda and ensures that policies turn into reality. He knows he is dealing with a sluggish system, therefore he keeps motivating the nation and the government machinery by constantly telling them about whatever has been achieved. In a way he updates the nation. He takes stock of things in public.

Speaking at the US's Council on Foreign Relations he enumerated his Jan Dhan Yojana, an initiative to give finanicial access to the poor, giving due credit to the bank officers,

> Our bank officials have gone door to door to open accounts for the poor. In less than five months, 14 crore accounts have been opened. Now the money will go directly to the poor. It is a huge record, acknowledged by the Guinness authorities—opening the maximum number of accounts in the shortest possible time. I asked banks to open accounts with a zero deposit. Look at the spirit our poor have, they have already put Rs 14,000 crore into bank accounts.

Addressing a workshop of BJP MPs at Delhi he explained to them the importance of nuclear energy, how difficult it is to get nuclear technology and fuel from the Western world and his personal efforts to get these for the nation: 'I went to Germany to attend the Hanover fair for Make in India. France has agreed to give us nuclear technology and Canada will give us nuclear technology and fuel for five years.' At such forums he keeps his style very informal, as he is speaking to his own party people.

Talking of corruption and several of his new policies and achievements at the same workshop he noted,

> When we say that after seventy-five years of Independence each man should have a home, are we doing this for the benefit of the rich? If we say that the previous government did nothing, are we at fault? Is the country not beset by corruption? If we say so then we are at fault! A bag of cement now sells for Rs 150, it was Rs 350 earlier. We have done this and shown them [the previous government].

Referring to the cooking-gas subsidy he said,

> Four lakh people have surrendered their gas subsidy. The Rs 200 crore that will accrue from this will not go to the government but will go towards lighting chullahs in the homes of the poor. Now they won't need to use coal or wood any more, and that will benefit the environment. If one crore part with their subsidy then one crore poor people will be able to use cooking gas.

Making a very valid point regarding freebies being given to the poor by various erstwhile governments he said, '*Rajneeti kehti hai free main do, lekin rashtraneeti kehti hai ke logon ke pas paisa ho jisse unki buying power badhey. Isse economy ko bhi protsahan milega.*' (Politics impels us to give freebies, but nationalism urges us to increase the buying power of the people by ensuring the money reaches the poor and by augmenting their income. This will also boost the economy.)

Talking about Swachh Bharat (Clean India) he said,

> People say, is this the job of a prime minister, to get toilets made? But I am an ordinary man, and I take care of the small things too. Dirt and lack of cleanliness are linked to a mindset. We have to change it, we have to change this

attitude. Foreign Minister Sushmaji sent some photographs of some embassy, before and after a cleanliness campaign. There was a lot of difference between the two. The thinking has to change.

About his achievements in Gujarat as a CM he says,

> *Hamare aadmi ke pass health card nahi hai. Lekin hamne Gujarat main har kisan ke pass soil health card diya hai, jo usey batata hai ki uski zamin par kaisi fasal sahi rahegi. Humne 6 lakh structures paani bachane ke liye banaye, desh bhar mein water table neeche ja raha hai, Gujarat mein wo upar aa raha hai. More crop per drop ka mera nara hai aur main 44 degree ki garmi main har saal Krish Mahotsav karta hoon. Pehle Gujarat main 23 lakh cotton bale banti thi, aab 1 crore 23 lakh bale banti hain. Textile to fibre, fibre to fabric, fabric to fashion, and fashion to foreign—ek complete chain honi chahiye.*(Our people don't have health cards. But in Gujarat I have given every farmer a soil health card, which tells him what crop would be ideal for his land. We have built 6 lakh structures to save water—throughout India, the water levels are going down but in Gujarat they are going up. My motto is 'More crop per drop' and I hold a farmers' festival every year in 44 degrees Celsius heat. Earlier 23 lakh bales of cotton used to be made, now 1 crore 23 lakh bales are made. Textile to fibre, fibre to fabric, fabric to fashion and fashion to foreign—there should be a complete chain.)

Comparing the performance of his government with that of the previous one, and taking them on accountability, he placed the facts in front of the people very clearly. 'If the UPA government issued 7 crore Aadhaar cards in forty-five months, we issued 17 crore in nine months. MNREGA [gave employment to] 5,000 people in forty-five months, we did 8 lakh in nine months. You gave a guarantee of 100 days but worked an average of 42.5 days in 2013–14. You spent 1 lakh crore but there's no audit of this.'

Talking about centre-state relations he said, '*Azadi ke baad pehli baar, budget ka 62% states ko jayega aur 38% centre ke pass rahega. Hum cooperative federalism chahate hai. Main mukhya mantri ki takleef samjhata hoon. Desh safal tab hoga jab states safal hongi.*' (For the first time after Independence, 62 per cent of the budget will go to the states and 38 per cent will stay with the centre. The country will prosper only when the states prosper.)

Speaking to the Indian diaspora at Toronto, he explained the significance of the colours of the national flag, and linked it to his achievements and strategy.

> Our flag has four colours—saffron, white, green and blue. Saffron symbolizes energy. Earlier we would talk only in terms of megawatt; now we talk of gigawatts. We need clean energy because we are responsible for one-sixth of the global warming. We need 175 gigawatt energy. To save energy, earlier the government bought LED bulbs at Rs 350 [per piece] and we now buy them at Rs 85 [per piece].

He then asked, '*Kyun bhaiyon, transparency ayi ya nahin ayi?*' (Is there transparency now or not?)

Addressing Delhi University students he talked about new avenues in education and said, 'Gujarat had eleven universities, today it has forty-four. We have started the first University of Forensic Science, the first in the world; the Raksha Shakti University for training people to join the police; a new institute for teachers' education. Can we export teachers or not? Teachers influence generations.'

Motivating a young audience he pointed out, 'We are a

big market; people dump their stuff on us. We should instead become a great manufacturing country and dump our goods on the world. We have to change our attitude. In Japan I saw slogans for the Olympics on almost everything, from biscuits to crockery. The slogan was, "Are we not ready to host the Olympics?" What did we do during the Commonwealth?'

Taking a dig at the opposition he said, 'Even those who worked did not know what or why they did.' He noted that those who wanted to do things did a lot, and said, 'I launched Vibrant Gujarat and in ten days we could have 121 countries participating—almost 50 per cent of the gross domestic product (GDP) of the world was under one roof.' Addressing the Indian diaspora in US and Toronto he announced, 'We will soon merge OCI (Overseas Citizen of India) and PIO (Person of Indian Origin). There is no need to go to the police station every fifteen days.'

Congratulating the ISRO scientists at the successful Mars Orbiter Mission (MOM), he said,

> MOM and Mars have met. MOM never lets you down. For the first time in history a mission has succeeded in the first attempt. You have created history. And this was done in record time—three years after the feasibility report. ISRO now joins an elite group of three countries. Parts were made by small factories in India. Let me tell you, that morning I had two choices, will the mission succeed or not. Let me assure you if it had failed I would have definitely been here. If plans are auspicious (mangal), then success is also auspiciously assured.

Paving the road ahead he said,

Failure draws criticism, and if you are successful then you are the target of envy and jealousy. Your success throws new challenges. You have to now train the next generation. The guru-shishya parampara (teacher-student relationship tradition) must be maintained. You have honoured our forefathers and inspired the next generation. We can change lives as space technology generates applications across multiple domains. We must now move from space technology to space application. We must have a SAARC satellite. We must push our boundaries to achieve more.

In the end he fired his motivational salvo by saying, 'When our cricket team wins, the whole nation dances. This is a thousand times more significant. Tomorrow is the auspicious day of Navratri, every school must celebrate this victory.'

When he was greeted by the Indian diaspora at Toronto, Canada, with chants of 'Modi! Modi!' in the auditorium, he said,

You with your hard work have earned respect in Canada which became a partner country in 2003 at the Gujarat Summit, and still remains one. We have great ties with this nation. You can come to Canada by air within seventeen hours, but it has taken forty-two years for an Indian prime minister to come. What was not done in forty-two years has been done in ten months.

Talking about the victory of his party and the involvement of Indians in Canada he said, 'The elections were taking place there, slogans were being shouted here. Results were being declared there and sweets were being distributed here.' Making a point, raising his index finger in the air, he said, 'There is just one solution to the whole problem,' and paused for effect before saying, 'It is not Modi; it is development. We have strength, we just need a chance. We have 260 crore hands. What can we not do? We can turn this nation into a golden bird. By 2030 the workforce for the entire world will be from India. We have to become Skill India from Scam India.'

After he became the PM, at the Vibrant Gujarat Summit on 11 January 2015, where more than 100 countries participated, he said,

> Someone's dreams depend on someone's directions. This is [a] meeting of hearts and minds. Problems present opportunities We want planet earth to be a safe and healthy place to live. India is not of today, it has a legacy that is thousands of years old. It is not a few cities, it has towns and lakhs of villages. We must work on culture, ethics and values. Yoga has been accepted by 177 countries and we will have 21 June as World Yoga Day.

Modi's greatest ability is that he doesn't refer to notes, yet he can quote facts, churn out figures and numbers with ease. He has all his facts and figures on his fingertips. He is gifted with a very powerful and photographic memory.

A powerful memory, along with the ability to correlate incidences for the right occasion and at the right time for the right audience, allows a speaker to deliver a mesmerizingly authentic speech every time he speaks. Reciting figures and statistics lends validity to the speech, which empty rhetoric can't achieve. For a prime minister to remember so many facts and figures along with his gruelling work schedule is no easy task.

The following examples illustrate this ability.

He demonstrated a razor-sharp memory by remembering

the names of all the guests, including the UN general secretary and several prime ministers who attended the Vibrant Gujarat Summit.

Speaking at the BJP workshop he said, 'Yemen had 24 hours' bombardment; we could block it for just two hours and bring thousands of Indians safely back. This is not a small incident. I salute General V.K. Singh, he stood there and got it done. Sushma Swaraj reacted in ten minutes and with these efforts thousands of nurses and the poor were evacuated.'

At Delhi University he said, 'In Gujarat we held 2,500–3,000 animal health camps to eradicate 120 cattle-related diseases. Milk production has gone up by 80 per cent. Gujarat was never a tourist destination, now the tourist numbers have doubled.'

In the Rajya Sabha he announced an accident insurance policy where he had all the numbers memorized. 'At Rs 330 per annum, or less than Rs 12 per month, you get accident cover of Rs 2 lakh. The Atal Pension Yojna at Rs 248 per annum for twenty years gives Rs 5,000 per month as pension after sixty years' age. If both husband and wife die, children get Rs 8.5 lakh back.'

Narendra Modi has the ability to connect facts with rhetoric. He says the right thing at the right time. Every person who wants to become a good speaker must learn to use facts and figures effectively.

Presenting a Grand Strategic Vision

One major leadership trait is to share a vision with all the stakeholders. A leader may be working hard and have great ideas, but he will never succeed if he doesn't share his vision and plans with his team and his workers. That is why great leaders like Narayana Murthy, Jim Collins and Steve Jobs shared their views in 'town hall' meetings.

Modi is brilliant at sharing his vision and aspirations and sounds very passionate and committed. Again, perception is very important. Communication must build perception. One often hears from people, 'Oh, here is a prime minister who we are proud of. We respect him because he knows what he is doing; he knows how to do it.' His speeches are full of hope.

As a leader of the largest democracy, he knows that there are thousands of problems but he also knows there are thousands of solutions and good things that can be done, if he wants to do them. Talking about the Jan Dhan Yojna he says, 'We have taken care of other unities but never talked about financial unity. We have to have financial inclusion; everyone must have a bank account.' Calling competition the key to progress, he says we need cooperative competitive federalism. States must compete with each other, only then will we progress.

'Making policies is not enough, we must ensure they are implemented. Reforms are no end in themselves; they must be backed with objectives. Big-ticket and small projects are both important.'

Talking about his policy and strategic intent he said,'What I am doing now will take some time. If I had done this in the last year of my tenure people would say, "Oh, they are on their way out, now nothing will happen".'

Addressing the India–US business summit on 26 January 2015 he explained,

> The road ahead is long, but we have worked tirelessly to build the economy, quality of life and Mother Nature. It will not happen overnight but we can do it because we have energy of youth, enterprise of business and optimism of a

nation. We will provide a predictable and conducive regime, will address uncertainties. Protect your intellectual property. [The] Scale and dream is vast, opportunity is huge. Railways, clean Ganga, urban waste management; 6,000,000 villages have to go digital, there is the need to make 5 million dwelling units in the next seven years. We don't require only strategy, we need enterprise, innovation, investment and imagination. We will be the major anchor for world stability, with 800 million young Indians. There are 3 million Indian Americans. Indian IT Companies are providing jobs in the US, and there are 100,000 Indian students in the US. As the two largest democracies we have a fundamental stake in each other's success. If we win together it will be a greater success.

Speaking to schoolchildren, he had a vision and a mission for them: 'Can you go and teach poor children one hour in a week? How do we make education a national priority? You must sweat four times a day to remain healthy. Will you do it? You must read biographies. We need all types of books, we also learn from history. Google doesn't give you knowledge, it gives only information.'

Addressing the Economic Times Global Summit he said, 'We have created an Expenditure Commission to get more bang for the buck. We must know where we are spending. We need to computerize the public distribution system so that ration supply is computerized and there is no pilferage.'

Addressing the Rajya Sabha he presented some of his ideas: 'The northeastern states are English-speaking. Why don't we make a big BPO industry there? Gold is dead money. We have 20,000 tonnes of gold. We can use it to give a boost to the economy by issuing gold bonds for depositing gold with the bank, which can be put to great use.'

At UNESCO, Paris, while addressing 1,300 diplomats he said:

> Our [Indian] Constitution is about culture and openness. It is not only cold statistics of growth but also the warm glow of belief and hope. We will protect the rights of every citizen and every religion. We will provide skill and education to every child. We will need 175,000 megawatts of clean energy in the next seven years. We also need to change our lifestyle for the sake of public health and we are going to celebrate World Yoga Day on 21 June every year.

In Parliament he strikes a brilliant chord with his commonsensical approach and spectacular rhetoric, as in the speech below.

> India is a nation of great people who made sacrifices. One person stood up against foreign rule and happily sacrificed his life for the nation. Then another one came and did the same thing. This went on and on, but did not get us freedom, because they were all individuals. Mahatma Gandhi was alone but he made it into a Jan Andolan, a People's Movement. He linked every activity, every work with freedom. Every teacher who taught in school taught for freedom. A factory worker felt he was contributing to freedom. For changing our nation and our progress, government programmes will fail. It has to be a Jan Andolan, only then will it succeed. At Mahatma Gandhi's 150 anniversary can't we offer a Swachh Bharat to show our respect? We have launched a clean-up campaign for this purpose.

Using motivational rhetoric typical to him, he says, 'I didn't get a chance to die for my country, but I can take a chance to live for it.' Committing himself to hard work and dedication he told the students of Delhi University, 'We spend years on paperwork. We need to move fast. We need skilled manpower. For progress it has to be skill, scale and speed.'

Mastering the Art of Oratory

Narendra Modi is not only a master craftsman of words, but has also mastered the art of mixing, with panache, hard facts and rhetoric.

He cleverly and clearly puts across the current state of affairs, pointing out weaknesses, then goes on to list out what all has been achieved in the same speech. Thereafter he elucidates his vision, his strategy and methodology to get things done and enumerates the means of fulfilling his promise. He demonstrates a unique ability to move back and forth to convey shortcomings, his achievements and his vision. He has clearly mentioned that one has to create an 'echo' effect so that people get to know about his personal commitment and that of his government.

Oratory is all about the 'echo' effect, it's all about perception because perception is reality as far as public speaking is concerned. Perception is all about influencing people, convincing people. Facts, conviction and eloquence need to be judiciously mixed.

LESSONS FROM A BRILLIANT LEADER AND SPEAKER

- Logic and facts juxtaposed with rhetoric and emotion can become a potent force to sway public opinion, even while dealing with the most stubborn audience. Facts and figures cannot be easily refuted and therefore act like a Teflon shield protecting an orator.
- Narendra Modi combines logic, satire, humour and emotions to produce a beautiful symphony to tell the people—'where we are, where we can go and how we can do it'. Every aspiring speaker has to learn this art.
- A person is able to present stark realities only with a heap of statistics. For the first time the nation learnt that 4.25 lakh toilets were required to take care of sanitation. As PM, he had the audacity to say that our graduates are unemployable. He said that the nation requires 175 gigawatts of energy, which can be managed only by nuclear energy. Figures define the enormity of a problem.
- Wrong perceptions can be set right with facts. Modi once told the Rajya Sabha that Goa and Nagaland have a large population of Christians, J&K had Muslims and Punjab had Sikhs; yet all these states have BJP or allied Governments, then how can one say that the BJP is a Hindu party?
- A good speaker identifies real problems and presents his case backed up by facts and figures. Modi talked about 5.5 crore people who do small-time business and employ a couple of people, generating 11 crore jobs. He urged the government to evolve a scheme which could help finance such small entrepreneurs. MUDRA is what emerged out of this analysis.

- Progress is reflected and measured by numbers, and not rhetoric or emotions. Modi informs his listeners about achievements with facts and figures. For example, he informed them that earlier Gujarat produced 23 lakh bales of cotton, and now it produces 1 crore 23 lakh bales per annum. These figures are very impactful.
- A good orator is also a good observer as is clear from Modi's observation of Japan's preparation for the Olympics.
- Great leaders make big announcements that demonstrate action like Modi who, while addressing the Indian diaspora in the US and Canada, made an announcement that his government would soon merge OCI and PIO, which was a long-standing demand. A speaker must utilize opportunities to announce good intentions and show achievements.

5

BECOME A GRANDMASTER

Stories, Similes, Slogans and Rhetoric

'The difference between the right word and the almost right word is the difference between lightning and a lightning bug.'
—Mark Twain

Great orators have the knack of picking up and narrating anecdotes from history to prove a point. Anecdotes help in establishing an instant connect with the audience. Anecdotes and stories are the best and most effective way of adding spice and life to a dialogue. When narrated by an orator, these substantiate the orator's point of view.

Anecdotes are very effective because they make the interaction between speaker and audience a little informal, a little more personal. A great speaker can break the barrier between him and the audience using simple and effective anecdotes. Leaders and orators who want to simplify their presentations must use anecdotes which people can easily relate to. The bottom line is that anecdotes make the speaker look genuine.

You're much 'more believable if you talk in your own voice', said author Maeve Binchy. Anecdotes drawn from your own experience can be effectively used to convey a point.

Modi comes up with great 'one-liners'—short but catchy phrases, which remain with the audience for a long time.

Successful lawyers also come up with anecdotes to convince the jury or substantiate their point of view.

Abraham Lincoln, while pleading a case before a jury, is said to have realized that he was going to lose the case, though his client was innocent. He is then said to have narrated the following anecdote:

> A farmer was sitting on the porch, when his six-year-old boy suddenly ran up and said, 'Father, the man you hired is in the barn with my sister. He is pulling down his trousers and sister is lifting up her skirt. I fear they are going to pee on the hay and spoil it!' The farmer said, 'Son, you have all the facts right but you have reached the wrong conclusion!'

The jury laughed aloud and Lincoln won his case. Similarly, parables were used by Jesus for his teachings, while further East Zen stories are also a powerful source to inspire and influence people. They can be effectively used within relevant contextual frameworks to reach out to the audience.

Stories and anecdotes which invoke human emotions make presentations memorable. People forget facts but seldom forget a nice, crisp story. And the beauty is that once they remember the story, they automatically recollect the fact linked with it. So the big picture is never lost. And that is the ultimate aim of a great speech. It should not only create an impact at that moment, but must have lasting effect on the audience.

Types of Stories to Choose

Stories and emotions work together to create lasting images in the mind. According to Nick Morgan, a communication theorist, there are five types of stories/quotes/slogans:

1. The 'quest' type of stories that inspire people to conquer, to work hard for a goal which appears very much within reach.
2. 'Stranger in the land' stories that project a hero who can turn things around, he emerges as a saviour in a hopeless situation.
3. 'Rags to riches' stories which talk about people from humble backgrounds who made it big. Such stories motivate an ordinary man to work for an ambitious goal and generate hope.
4. The 'love story' format which talks about love-hate relationships, where there is collaboration between organizations, or relationships between people, going through ups and downs on the way to resolution.
5. A 'tale of revenge' that motivates people to settle scores. Getting justice for the wronged.

A great orator picks up the right kind of story for the right kind of audience and the right context. As a master craftsperson, he then fits in these at the right place within his secret.

Narendra Modi very intelligently picks up stories, slogans and some hard-hitting expressions and anecdotes to illustrate his points.

Taking the rags-to-riches format he talks about his poor background and yet demonstrates that he has become the PM. He urges people to share his grand economic view of making the economy tenfold.

He has often talked about himself as *'samanya warg ka aadmi, ek chai bechne wala vyakti'*. His personal story motivates the common man and earns him respect. Using the 'love story' format he has often said about the opposition in Parliament, *'Hamare kitne bhi mat bhed hon, hame saab ko sath lekar chalna hai.'* He says, *'Hame apni ego, apne abhiman ko door rakhna hoga.'* He very often motivates people with anecdotes that inspire them to conquer: *'Kya hum is desh ki economy ko 2 trillion se 20 trillion tak nahin le ja sakte hain? Kya hum apni 1.25 crore ki democracy ko ek takat ke roop main duniya ke samne nahin rakh sakte?'*

The Art of Storytelling

Narendra Modi has mastered the art of weaving short stories and anecdotes into his speeches. He usually uses personal experiences and narrates them as stories to demonstrate conviction and is able to drive home his point very effectively and convincingly.

Talking of the Gujarat model and lauding the aspirations of a farmer in the remote corners of India, he narrated an anecdote, while addressing the students of Delhi University at the Shri Ram College of Commerce (SRCC):

> There is a tribal belt near the Maharashtra border, which I frequently visited when I was not in politics. Farmers from that area later visited me and said, 'Please do something about our roads.' I responded by saying, 'But you do have decent tar roads, then what is the problem?' They replied, 'Yes there are good tar roads but we still need some improvement. We grow export quality bananas which are exported to Finland. When our bananas are sent by trucks,

> 20 per cent of our produce is damaged because the ride is not very smooth. We want paver[1] roads.'

Modi went on to explain, 'Friends, even places like Delhi do not have paver roads. Just think about the foresight of these farmers and their aspirations even in tribal areas. If my fellow citizens can aspire to do so much, then I can clearly see a bright future for my country.'

He went on to say that great aspirations and a desire to do well is the hallmark of success. No country can progress until and unless it thinks big, it desires more. Our time has come and we will now do big things.

To illustrate this point, Modi went on to talk about South Korea and its achievements. 'A nation that obtained independence after us has hosted the Olympics. And when they hosted the games, the whole world was amazed. That was the turning point for South Korea. People acknowledged that South Korea as a nation had arrived; its time had come.'

To substantiate the fact that India is now poised to become a power to reckon with, and also that people view India differently, while addressing students of Delhi University he said,

> We need to take on the world with self-confidence. We are not inferior to anyone in the world… When President Bill Clinton came to India he visited a village near Jaipur; he saw for himself how women were running a computer centre.

---

[1] A paver (paver finisher, asphalt finisher, paving machine) is a piece of construction equipment used to lay asphalt on roads, bridges, parking lots and other such places. It lays the asphalt flat and provides minor compaction before it is compacted by a roller. Source: https://en.wikipedia.org/wiki/Paver_(vehicle)

> During this visit a Dalit boy came out of nowhere and went up to Clinton to speak to him. Everyone was shocked and concerned. They were worried he would say something silly and shame them. But this boy said something which pleasantly surprised the whole nation. He asked the president, which the whole world saw on TV, 'Mr Clinton, do you still think my country is backward? Do you still think of it as drowned in poverty and superstition?' When the interpreter translated it, Clinton responded by saying, 'No, I don't believe this now. Wherever I go to, I will tell the world, what India really is.'

Narendra Modi has the knack of connecting the dots in a different way. He can easily rattle out an impactful event in a story format. His short stories, incidents and anecdotes are very effective. He is able to relate his stories very well within the context of his speeches.

He narrates incidents in the form of touching and motivating stories, giving a strong message that there are unassuming, simple and down-to-earth Indians who can work wonders and create world-class products in record time and under all odds. Here's one such.

> When I was CM of Gujarat, a young man came to see me one day. He was not very presentable, not impressive and had poor communication skills. He was Gujarati, born in Africa and had later moved to Canada and grown up there. We spoke for a few minutes but I thought he was wasting my time. So I told him to meet the collector of Baroda. I asked my PA to send him away as he was going to waste my time. My office informed the collector and this fellow left my office. After thirteen months this person came to my office again. My PA said, 'No, sir, he has come to invite you.' I said,

> 'An invitation? Oh send him in.' He came in and said, 'Sir I had met you earlier, now my factory is ready and I want you to inaugurate it.' I was astounded. This man whom I had dismissed, thinking he was useless, was inviting me for inauguration. I accepted the invitation. He also invited me for the product launch six months after that. You will be amazed. He came to meet me for the first time, inaugurated his factory in thirteen months, and six months after the start of the factory, launched his first product. And what product did he create? For the metros that you are so proud of in Delhi, I launched the coach of that metro train!

Here Narendra Modi also scores a point by telling the audience that he erred in his judgement, but the way he narrated the story also revealed him as an honest, well-meaning and great political leader to his audience. Here is a man, who was the chief minister of Gujarat for ten years, now a prime minister, and he admits that he could not appropriately assess a person who came to meet him. How many people in power would admit something like that in public? This is what the audience would think.

There is another simple yet touching story that he narrated when he was asked by a schoolgoing child during a question-answer session, 'How do people in politics handle pressure?'

Modi responded, 'Once a three-year-old boy was very tired and could not walk. His elder sister who was just five years old carried him on her back. She walked miles and miles in the scorching sun. A mahatma was watching all this and said "Are you not tired?" The girl said, "He is my brother and therefore I am not tired at all." I do not get tired because the 1.25 billion people of India are my family.'

Narendra Modi has motivated Indians by telling them about

their own achievements. He has never ever criticized industry; his criticism is reserved for the government machinery, the bureaucratic system and the opposition. He trains his guns at the opposition, the elite political class, and criticizes the sluggish government processes. This way he has positioned himself as, 'I am one of you, I know the pain. I have endured the pain and I am here to eradicate all that. I am here to demolish the archaic systems.'

Giving credit to the Indian software industry and our youth, Modi has narrated an interesting story to Indian audiences at home as well as abroad. This is the way a leader motivates the masses.

> Fifteen years ago I visited Taiwan. During my visit, I had an interpreter. By the time I finished my tour, we had become quite familiar. He therefore hesitantly asked me, 'Sir, if you don't mind, can I ask you a question?' I said, 'Yes, go ahead, what is that you want to ask me?' He asked, 'Do you still have snakes and snake charmers in your country? Do you still live in the world of spirits, ghosts and superstition?' I said, 'No, these days we have undergone devaluation.' He asked me what that meant and I said, 'Our ancestors used to be snake charmers, we have lost that ability and we are now mouse charmers.' Friends, our youngsters with their fingertips on the mouse of a computer have moved the world. This is the power of the youth; they have forced the world to look at India with a different lens.

Such a simple example in the form of a story kindles the hopes and aspirations of our youth. It boosts their self-esteem and brings a smile on their lips because the episode is humorous too.

Narendra Modi never misses an opportunity to narrate incidents that create great value in the minds of people. He is able to project himself as an inquisitive person who is hungry to learn.

Addressing Indians settled in China, at Shanghai, he narrated a story that not only had an impact on the audience but also delivered a diplomatic message of great significance:

> When I was elected as the prime minister, the president of China Mr Xi Jinping called me up to congratulate me. He told me that he had done some background study on me and knew exactly where I was born. When he came to India he visited Gujarat and wanted to visit my village but couldn't do so because of lack of time. [...] People are of the opinion that Mahatma Buddha had influence only across the eastern seaboard of India. But Chinese philosopher Xuan Zang, who visited India a long time ago, had visited my village Vadnagar and written a book in which he mentioned that an educational institute with a hostel facility had been built near Vadnagar, my village, for Buddhist monks. When I became the CM of Gujarat, I asked my government to undertake excavations in that area. To our surprise, we found all the hostels, buildings and artifacts that Xuan Zang had described in his book.
>
> Friends, President Xi Jinping, when I met him yesterday, told me that after visiting my village Vadnagar, Xuan Zang returned to China and visited his [the President's] village. There is a big Buddhist temple in his village, which finds mention in Xuan Zang's book. President Xi Jinping had kept that book and had marked that page, which he showed me. He said, 'Look, this is the name of your village and here is the name of my village, which Xuan Zung has written about.' When two heads of state share such feelings of brotherhood, such closeness, such warmth, this creates a great sense of understanding and confidence between two countries.

Further linking the discussion to the presence of the large number of Indians in China, he said, 'When you came to China, you must have had lot of apprehensions, about what Chinese eat, what are their customs. Haven't these been dispelled after you have come to China? The unity and brotherhood that you can create amongst people by two nations, neither Narendra Modi nor the ambassador can create.'

In one master stroke he connected the people of two nations, motivated Indians abroad and left a lasting message with the Chinese top brass that he wanted to build lasting, friendly and fruitful relations with them.

Very few political leaders and even corporate leaders today have mastered the art of weaving meaningful short anecdotes and personal experiences in a story form in their narrative. Narendra Modi has mastered the skills of a storyteller, which everyone aspiring to be a speaker must learn.

Using Similes and Comparisons in Speeches

Modi uses comparisons very effectively. For instance, 'We have to create a Jan Andolan for progress, like the Jan Andolan created by Mahatma Gandhi for Azadi.'

What if you have two great similes that essentially mean the same thing? For example, 'The water in the lake was as still as the hands of a surgeon', or 'The water in the lake was as still as a statue'. How do you know which to choose? Simple, whichever fits your context better. If you are narrating a story about a doctor then the former fits better. If you are using it in the context of an architect or a designer the latter fits better. While addressing spiritually inclined audiences you could tweak the same simile: 'The water in the lake was as still as the mind of a person in samadhi.'

Using Metaphors

Presentation and sales specialist Anne Miller notes, 'Imagery—the core of metaphoric language—will surprise, grab, inform and persuade your [reader] as mere explanation will not. Vivid language will distinguish you from the swarm, will make you heard above the drone, will make you that rare person today: a communicator who gets results.'[2]

For instance, Modi used an unusual metaphor to emphasize the role and power of yoga. He said, 'People buy mobile phones but never read the user manual given with it. Similarly, we don't know what God has given us. We have not read the user manual given to us. Yoga is a way to read that user manual.'

Metaphors help explain complex topics. They stimulate the right brain, the creative side of the brain, just as stories do. They thus demolish left-brain rationality and therefore manage to get the audience to lower their guard.

In simple words, metaphors are a simple way of thinking about or expressing something in terms of something else. For instance, Pablo Picasso linked the impact of art to everyday life when he said, 'Art washes away from the soul, the dust of everyday life,' and Kahlil Gibran linked a person's habitual speech to the thoughts that ran amok in their mind, though he put it very beautifully, 'All our words are but crumbs that fall down from the feast of the mind.' Such thought-provoking metaphors are hard to find.

At ISRO, while congratulating the scientists on the successful Mars mission, Modi said something very beautiful and close to every Indian heart, 'Today MOM met Mangal [the Hindi

---

[2] http://www.annemiller.com/default.asp

name for Mars], and Mangal got MOM.' This acronym MOM (Mars Orbiter Mission), was used by him very creatively when he said, 'MOM would never disappoint.'

Using Slogans and Quotes

Slogans

Slogans are essential to a narrative and can work wonders with a speech because they add that oomph factor. Slogans work well for politics, selling or branding products, advertising and even making a boardroom presentation. A slogan must have style and substance. Style is essential and in several cases substance is somewhat secondary. Style implies that a slogan must have zing to it and should sound right, should have easy recall and must be easy to say. Substance comes next in the pecking order, and the bottom line is that a slogan must be meaningful.

For instance the slogan, 'Yes, we can!', which catapulted Barack Obama to fame, has great style and good substance. Style is an art form and because getting the style right is entirely a matter of art, there is no formula which, if applied, can get you the right slogan. It is something like getting the right title for a book. It could also get as complex as looking for a formula for making a hit movie or coming up with a tune which makes a song an eternal hit. Why 'Besame Mucho' sung by Andrea Bocelli and written by Consuelo Velazquez in 1940 is still such a craze, or why 'It's a hard day's night' by The Beatles still rings a bell cannot be discussed or dissected by any of the music maestros.

Ultimately a slogan must be catchy and memorable. It should also be short and crisp.

'Britain deserves better' was a British Labour Party slogan

for the 1997 general elections; 'Don't mess with Texas' was the slogan of an anti-littering campaign in Texas, America; 'Better dead than red' was a powerful anti-Communist slogan; while 'Drill, baby drill' was used by Republican Party in the US to call for more domestic production of oil; and *'Tum mujhe khoon do. Main tumhe azadi doonga'* (You give me blood. I will get you freedom) by Subhas Chandra Bose was a powerful slogan during the Indian independence movement.

Some of Modi's memorable slogans include, 'Zero defect and zero effect', which urges industry to create products that have zero defects and zero effects on the environment. He has also defined India's strength in a catchy three-word slogan, 'Democracy. Demography. Demand.'

To motivate the agricultural sector he says 'more crop per drop'; to define India's large population and young manpower as our strength he calls it 'demographic dividend'.

Quotes and one-liners

These are usually meaningful statements which involve philosophical thoughts, whereas slogans are distinctive phrases or a cry which urges you to act and serves as a motto.

Narendra Modi has demonstrated the ability to create slogans as well as quotes that are high on style and convey his vision and intentions very clearly. Declaring his intention to serve he says, *'Main pradhan mantri nahin, pradhan sevak hoon'* (I am not the prime minister, I am the prime servitor), which has become a hugely quotable quote in Hindi. His slogan, 'More crop per drop,' urges farmers and scientists to work together to hike produce by minimizing and optimizing water usage.

Yet another impactful Modi quote is, 'I did not get an

opportunity to die for the country, but I have got an opportunity to live for the country'. Also popular is, 'The government has no business to be in business.'

Master of Rhetoric

'The art of effective or persuasive speaking or writing, especially the exploitation of figures of speech and other compositional techniques' is how the term rhetoric is usually defined.[3] A good orator is able to convey his point effectively and convince his audience of his sincerity by using rhetoric.

Political leaders like Winston Churchill, Harry S. Truman and several others used rhetoric to deliver some memorable and mesmerizing speeches.

'The Allied armies, through sacrifice and devotion and with God's help have wrung from Germany, a final and unconditional surrender,' said Harry Truman while announcing the surrender of Germany at the end of the Second World War.

Some great orators write their speeches themselves, while many depend on speech writers but ensure that their own ideas remain intact. Winston Churchill wrote all his own speeches, and in fact took pride in writing every word himself. He said he spent an hour working on every minute of a speech he made! People who have examined his art of creating speeches reveal the extraordinary creative process. 'His first draft looked like a normal typescript but the final draft was like a poem,' says Declan Kiely, curator of manuscripts at the Morgan Library, New York. Narendra Modi too has perfected the art of rhetoric and this is clearly visible in his simple and yet very convincing phraseology.

---

[3] http://www.oxforddictionaries.com/definition/english/rhetoric

While speaking in Madison Square Garden, New York, to the Indian diaspora he said, 'During the elections many of you couldn't vote. But the day the results came, you couldn't have slept.' This was given a resounding response by the audience with a chant, 'Modi, Modi, Modi.'

He waited for the din to subside and said, 'No political pundit could predict [the outcome]. Poor villagers vented their opinion of the opinion makers.' Reassuring the public of his commitment to perform he said,

> We will never let you down. We will not do anything because of which you have to look down or feel ashamed... It is a great responsibility. Since the time I became the PM, I have not even taken a fifteen-minute vacation. As a CM I said, anyone who has to come to India, come quickly. Now you also feel that you must have one foot in India.

In yet another rhetoric-filled salvo he enthralled the audience by saying, 'America is the oldest democracy and India is the largest democracy. *Saari duniya ke log America main basey hain aur Bharat ke log duniya ke har desh main basey hain.*' (People from around the world live in America and people from India can be found everywhere in the world.)

Applauding the contribution of Indians in America he said, 'You eat the same food that we do, you drink the same water that we do. If you can do all this then why can't we?'

Applauding India's scientific community for a successful Mars mission, he said, 'In Gujarat if you travel by autorickshaw the fair is ten rupees per kilometre, but friends, we have achieved Mission Mars at seven rupees per kilometre. That is less than the budget of a Hollywood film. And we have achieved this in our first attempt.' This was a brilliantly simple example of our achievement as a nation.

Talking about financial inclusion he said, 'Our banks were nationalized a long time ago, still 50 per cent of the people don't have bank accounts; a poor man still goes to loan sharks to take a loan.'

Giving a call to the entrepreneurs he said, 'Don't become job seekers, become job creators.'

Talking about good governance he said, 'Earlier the government took pride in making laws, but I want to demolish old laws and as many laws, so that the system becomes more simplified.'

Referring to the way he had made government functioning more effective and responsive he said, 'I read some news articles that government officers now come to the office on time. Do you think this is a news item? I feel very upset and pained when I see this.' He thus scored a point about having made government servants more accountable, whilst also pointing out that all other governments had not been able to achieve this and that is why, for Indian people, it was great news.

In the US he asked, 'Do you all want to bathe in the Ganges? Should our Ganga be clean? Every countryman must help. Will you all help?'

The people in the audience responded with fervour and cries of, 'Modi!' 'Modi!'

Cleaning the Ganga is a difficult job and he said, 'People ask me, why are you taking up such difficult jobs? I tell them, you didn't elect me to do small and easy jobs.'

Great leaders sense the times and tides, they sense the public mood, they can sense the seriousness of the problems, of the situation and this is reflected as brilliant rhetoric in their speeches. When Hitler's armies were demolishing country after country in Europe, Winston Churchill told Britons and the Allies the truth. On 13 May 1940 he said, at the House of Commons, 'I have nothing to offer but blood, toil, tears and sweat,' These words went down in history and the Allies themselves rewrote history after the Second World War. Churchill presented the truth in front of his people in the most straightforward way.

Narendra Modi has also used similar methods to tell people what the reality is. Addressing the civil servants on Civil Services Day he said, 'Till 2001, drought or floods were the only two calamities which were viewed by us as disasters. These impacted our agriculture. The Gujarat earthquake showed us that disasters can also hit the common man and we had to look at disasters beyond agriculture.'

Addressing the students at SRCC, he delivered a rhetorical punch by saying, 'People look at a glass as half full or half empty. I have a third way of looking at it. The glass is half full and the rest is full of air.' He was rewarded by thunderous applause.

Addressing the US Business Summit on 26 January 2015, in the presence of President Barack Obama, he said, 'We are the two largest democracies and your [President Obama's] visiting India twice in a short time is a testimony to the transformation of our relationship. We are entering into a critical partnership with greater frequency of participation. There is going to be a hotline between President Obama and me.'

In all his speeches Modi tries to motivate Indians to realize their own potential, telling them that even after a seemingly hopeless situation there is great hope that the nation can march forward.

Addressing the Indian Diaspora at Toronto, Modi captured the imagination of Indian Canadians by saying,

> The elections were going on there [in India], but slogans for support were being shouted here. Results were being declared there and sweets were being eaten here; they were celebrating during the day there, and here at night.
>
> *Log bolte hain sarkar badli to kya badla. Dus mahine ke baad janata ka mann bhi badla.* (People say what has changed after the government has changed? In ten months people's minds have changed.)

Then Modi quoted a famous Hindi film song, '*Dekh tere insaan ki halat, kya hogai bhagwaan, kitna badal gaya insaan.*' He went on to say,

> *Ab insaan kitna accha ho gaya hai.* I asked banks to open accounts for the poor with zero deposit. *Bank ke officers bhi badal gaye, sau din main 14 crore account khol diye. Jo ki teen Canada ke barabar hai. Garib ke pas paisa nahin hai per, garib ki aamiri ki taquat dekho, 14,000 crore rupaya jama kara diya. Sarkar badli to jaan maan badla hai.* (Now man has become so good. I asked banks to open accounts for the poor with zero deposit. Even bank officers have changed, they opened 14 crore accounts in hundred days, which is equal to [the population of] three Canadas. Poor people have no money but look at their spirit, they deposited 14,000 crores in these accounts. The government has changed and people have also changed.)

Modi's speeches are all persuasive, if not ubiquitous.

Great oratory and eloquence rely heavily on stories, similes, metaphor and rhetoric. How these are intertwined with the rest of the context and within the context is a fine art.

Very few orators in the world, and virtually none from the Indian political scenario, have been able to use oratory and exploit it to motivate a nation and win over the people as has Narendra Modi. He has set a new benchmark for a positive rhetoric in the political arena.

ORATORY AND LEADERSHIP LESSONS FROM A BRILLIANT SPEAKER

- Great orators make their speeches come alive by narrating stories from history, as well as from their own life. They use similes, slogans and quotes to substantiate their point of view. They break the barrier between themselves and their audience, sharing their personal experiences using anecdotes.
- Effective orators pick up the right type of stories and anecdotes, which fit into their overall scheme of things and the message that they intend to deliver. Narendra Modi has mastered the art of picking up appropriate anecdotes and stories, which he uses very effectively to address very diverse types of audience.
- Using similes is an art which every potential speaker must learn. Great speakers know what the objects of desire are for a particular target audience. Similes need to be doctored according to the audience and the context of the speech.
- Slogans are a great way to pump fire into a speech. Good slogans have strong recall value and can create brand equity for a speaker. A slogan must have zing to it, should sound good and must be easy to recall. A powerful slogan not only makes a lot of sense, but has the quality of recall.
- Picking the right story is the easier part of preparing a speech. The more difficult part is the way the story is delivered. This part has more to do with dialogue delivery and a bit of enactment. After all, stories are used by orators to draw the attention of their audience and then to keep them engrossed for the rest of the discourse—Narendra Modi does this brilliantly.

- Speakers like Winston Churchill, Harry Truman and John Kennedy mastered the art of rhetoric. They were the most persuasive speakers of the last century. They could convince their audience by exploiting figures of speech and other compositional techniques. With practice they learnt how to sound genuine and honest in front of millions. All those who want to become effective orators must listen to speeches delivered by them.

6

FEROCITY OF HOPE

Philosophy. Strategy. Action. Simplicity

'We must accept finite disappointment, but never lose infinite hope.'
—Martin Luther King, Jr

Most of us get ideas, but how many of us have the ability to articulate them in simple words and put them in front of millions in a manner that inspires and creates hope?

Modi's philosophy, his ideas and his approach to solving complex problems has brought a whiff of fresh air to the Indian political arena and hope to the largest democracy in the world, raising the aspirations of millions.

He has changed the way people look at the political class, which, in the last almost seventy years of Independence, mostly had nothing new to offer. People were fed up of a leadership which couldn't inspire confidence; they were sick and tired of the same dialogues repeated by the political class, minus results.

Needless to say, every political leader and party is constantly under public scrutiny and every sentiment and idea is under the scanner by the media, which loves to debate everything under the sun. In such circumstances a leader/party needs to be sure-footed, confident and, above all, gutsy to the core, which Modi is. He displays clarity of thought and speedy, decisive action.

Solutions: From Outside the Box or Within It?

Out-of-the-box thinking is a management expression, which means to think differently or unconventionally. People who view problems differently and are able to provide unique solutions rather than run-of-the-mill ones, are people who have creative minds.

As they say, 'necessity is the mother of invention'. In the solution-provider context, out-of-the-box thinkers are the real inventors. They may not invent a machine, but they do invent solutions. Such people are not only creative but are also bold enough to challenge the status quo—one of the most sought-after qualities of a good leader. A good leader challenges the status quo when he believes that something different needs to be done to find solutions.

There may be very few political leaders in contemporary history who have demonstrated such clarity of thought as has Narendra Modi's. He thinks out of the box, uses common sense and presents simple yet workable solutions. He applies his mind and heart with equal enthusiasm to problems that appear to be as elusive and big as black holes, as well as to those which appear to be child's play.

Inside-the-box thinkers, on the other hand, restrict their thought processes to conventional ways of looking at things. They go by what has been done previously; following conventions, rulebooks and historically accepted guidelines to seek solutions—their mind is thus locked up in an imaginary box; hence they 'think inside the box'.

Leadership Is All About Thinking Straight

Modi thinks on his feet and provides clear and precise solutions on the go. His head appears to be full of ideas and strategies to resolve the problems that India has been grappling with since Independence.

He demonstrates that he has it in him—always and every time. No one has been able to challenge, leave aside criticize, his strategic thinking. His philosophy, 'Team India', is above board and hard-hitting.

Unlike many speakers who often forget the power of saying something different to their audience, laying greater emphasis on tone and/or body language than on context and content, Modi delivers a different flavour every time to the audience, whether it be the public, a gathering of scientists or a collection of bureaucrats.

When orators like Modi, who are known to deliver spectacular speeches one after the other, come up on stage, TV or radio, the audience thinks, 'Let us see what he has to say this time.' There is a sense of expectancy, a sense of anticipation, which builds excitement even before the speaker reaches the mike.

Narendra Modi demonstrates this ability to pull the rabbit out of the hat, almost every time. He is a thinker of a calibre that India has never seen in its contemporary history. With his revolutionary thought process, which he beautifully articulates, he has touched millions of hearts.

Modi, as PM, has also applied his mind to all facets of governance and addressed problems that plague every segment of society, every sector of industry and every age group simultaneously. The first thing he has done as prime minister is to create a culture of responsiveness, punctuality and discipline in the top brass.

Giving a speech to the secretaries to the Government of India, he motivated them to take quick and prompt decisions. He even shared his mobile number with them and encouraged them to get in touch in case they faced any difficulty.

Addressing the bureaucrats on Civil Services Day, 21 April 2015, he urged them to strike a proper work-life balance. He suggested that they spend time with their families and opined that to run such a big country, they needed to remain happy and fit. 'How can you work if you wilt?' he asked.

He suggested that they identify ten top projects every year and these should be discussed as award-winning projects. These should be seen by all and should become an opportunity to learn from. 'The kind of policies you make, the good things you do for the country will be more important than having cars and bungalows. Your own children will also measure you on these parameters,' he said.

In order to motivate the youth to join the civil services and attract maximum talent, he asked each civil servant to spare at least five days a year to teach in colleges and interact with students. 'Tell the youth what great work you are doing, what satisfaction you get out of this job, so that best talent comes to the civil services,' he added.

He also came up with the novel idea of felicitating retired civil servants who attain seventy-five years of age. 'We must learn from them,' he said, 'They are a great institutional memory, they have a lot of experiences.' He then suggested an institutional knowledge bank,

> Can we not make a system where right from a peon to a chief secretary everyone writes their own experiences, within two

to five pages, at the time of retirement? This will be a sharing of experience. It is like preserving history. Each such sharing can be uploaded on the cloud and should remain for posterity. The organization can benefit from this knowledge bank in a big way.

Illustrating his point he said,

> The British built big guest houses and circuit houses at a distance of every 20 kilometres. These were well-equipped and many had wood carvings and other facilities. Do you know why these were placed at every 20 kilometres? Because in those days British officers travelled by elephant or horses, and they could travel only this much in a day. Such knowledge comes out of history.

Addressing his party members at the BJP MPs' workshop in New Delhi on 19 April 2015, he demonstrated another example of his out-of-the-box thinking.

> When we come up with a scheme to give a gas cylinder to every poor person, even in the rural areas, people said, 'But they don't have tables to place their gas burners on; the burner will be placed on the floor and the cylinder next to it. So how will they use gas for cooking?' and I said, 'Dig a hole in the floor, place the gas cylinder in it and connect it to the burner on the floor!' It's that simple.

Resource Optimization

Spinning out an idea whilst dealing with the subject of agriculture, Modi said, 'We will buy damaged crop and use it the best way we can. This will reduce wastage.'

One of the reasons the man creates so much hope is because of this out-of-the-box attitude that shows us just how resource-rich we are. If it can be used, he will try to put it to use. Organizations fail because of dead resources. A great leader or a CEO can turn a loss-making organization into a profitable one by using the existing resources properly, and this creates hope. Narendra Modi has applied his mind to many such government resources, which are underutilized.

Talking about soil health cards for farmers, he said,

> We don't need new labs to do soil testing. We have school buildings and laboratories in every school. Let us train boys and girls from the villages to test soil. They can use the school labs after school hours to do this. This way we will create lakhs of entrepreneurs, we would create jobs and side by side the farmers will benefit from soil health cards. There is no need to create new labs.

As mentioned earlier in this book, on one occasion he said, 'There are thousands of railway stations where only one or two trains come every day. These railway stations have buildings, road connectivity, have electricity and water. Why can't we make skill development centres on these railway stations?' When people listen to such ideas they wonder why no one thought of them earlier.

This 'never waste resources' approach applies to official trips as well. Explaining the reason behind his visit to Japan in 2014 to members of the Lok Sabha he said, 'I went to Japan to meet a Nobel Laureate. I had just one purpose. I went there to meet Shinya Yamanaka—who is a stem-cell research pioneer and a 2012 Nobel Prize winner. Because sickle cell anaemia, which is widespread in India's tribal regions, must get stem cell research solutions. India and Japan can work together on this.'

He managed to spot an opportunity to partially solve the critical question of providing nutrition-rich food to the poor. Addressing Parliament, he noted, 'Bananas have the greatest nutrition value, and is the best fruit for the poor. Australia has a "super banana" lab, which is working on creating a variety that will be replete with Vitamin A and iron. Similarly, we would also like to learn from Australia how to grow dal and chana on the worst possible soils.'

He realizes the vast potential of India's geographical diversity. 'The Northeast has great potential for producing organic products,' he says. 'We must make it the organic capital of India. This will get the northeastern states on an equal footing with other states.'

Futuristic Thinking

Narendra Modi has understood the potential of information technology and wants 'digital inclusion' for all 1.25 billion Indians. He wants connectivity in such a way that every Indian can access information and interact with the government. He is sure that a connected India and technology will bring in transparency, reduce paperwork and make things easier for the people. It will prompt digital literacy and generate lakhs of jobs. He envisages that once everyone has a mobile, the country will be easy to govern. This is a project close to his heart and for which there is a private investment commitment of crores of rupees. This will generate jobs and will give connectivity to the whole nation. Giving an example he said, 'In Gujarat we automated the public distribution system. Sixteen lakh ghost cards were busted because of this. This is all because of technology.'

Modi backs his ideas with a proven track record. He automated fourteen toll collection stations located on Gujarat's borders with Maharashtra, Rajasthan and Madhya Pradesh, while the neighbouring states didn't do this. As a result, there was no pilferage and Gujarat collected Rs 2,000 crore more tax than the others.

Modi demonstrates the ability of leading from the front and dares to experiment. A man of action, he has the courage to implement his ideas.

While addressing the India Today Conclave in 2013, he said, 'If we want to become a global economy, we need to have excellent world-class ports. Just ports are not enough, they need to be connected with railways.' Criticizing the current political mindset he said, 'Due to political pressure during the Rail Budget the government is focused only on increasing number of passenger trains and adding coaches. No one thinks of increasing the number of trains, and the connectivity of the ports to the railway system, which is required to be done in a big way.'

Presenting the issue from another perspective, he asked,

> The government makes roads, but do private vehicles ply on them or not? Airports are built by the government but private aircraft use them. Then why do only government-owned trains run on railway tracks constructed by the government? We have two types—passenger and freight trains. Why can't we have another type? We can have 'parikrama' trains which connect religious destinations with big cities. There is a hundred crore market for this. Hindus want to visit temples located in some specific cities. Similarly, Muslims may like to visit Ajmer Sharif, Christians want to go to Goa and Sikhs to Amritsar. These could be thematic trains

> which can be privatized. We will generate revenue, use existing resources and provide a service to our citizens.

Modi also believes that we need to change the way we govern. 'Ideas need to be institutionalized. Leader-centric, personality-centric or individual-centric ideas will last for few years and then disappear,' he said.

Projecting a Fresh Perspective

A presenter or a speaker becomes an orator if he is able to project a fresh perspective. People soak in fresh ideas quickly. In fact, they look forward to hearing something new. Modi has the knack of putting things in the correct perspective and calls a spade a spade. He paints a picture which appears to be fresh and also offers a new perspective. Remember, your audience is aware of the realities, but they would like to hear it from you.

For instance, during the India Today Conclave in 2013, during the question-answer session Modi was asked, 'What is our biggest problem?'

He candidly replied, 'We are the biggest problem. Our mindset is our problem.' As though suggesting a solution, he went on to say,

> I see every calamity as an opportunity, we can change this mindset. We did this when Gujarat was hit by an earthquake. We learnt about disaster management and institutionalized processes and managed that calamity very well. We need to involve people, especially women; our power will double. We did an experiment where 25 lakh women were involved from the villages. They are now doing business of Rs 1,700 crore per annum, which in the near future will become Rs 5,000 crore.

Answering a question on eradication of corruption he said, 'We need to provide stability of tenure for government officers. When you transfer out a bad guy you are only transferring the problem. When you ask for a completion report, things start working. Corruption starts when you do favours by posting officers. There is not even one request that comes to my office in this regard.'

He further added, 'It has to start from the top. If you don't have vested interest you can do it.'

When told, 'But you need money to fight elections. How do you manage that?' he responded, 'It's not wrong to ask for donations. We collect money through donations. Problems arise when politicians ask for bribes through contracts. They ask for a 10 per cent cut and don't bother even if the bridge is sub-standard. But by accepting donations, we get notes and votes too.'

He went on to present a different perspective on managing electricity shortage in rural areas,

> Unfortunately, we operate everything in a sarkari (bureaucratic) manner. That is why we can't find a solution. Can you reduce farmers' electricity supply? Absolutely not, they will start protesting. *Kisano ko main bijli kam dunga, yeh kehne mein rajniti mein takat lagti hai.* (I will give less electricity to farmers; to say this you need a lot of guts if you are in politics.) We have found a unique solution to this. I told the farmers to focus on water rather than electricity. In Gujarat there is a drought for seven years out of ten. We have started micro irrigation.

Explaining good governance he said,

> In the corporate world you have brainstorming. *Ham har saal chintan shibir kartey hain aur 250 se 300 officer teen din*

ke liye kahin jatey hain. Isse kya accha hua? Approach badli. Jab ham pe angrez raj karte they to officers ka kaam tha British saltanat ko khush rakhna. Aaj hum independent country hain. Officers ko sarkar ko khush karne ke liye kaam nahin karna, balki, janta ke liye kaam karna hai. (We hold a brainstorming session every year in which 250 to 300 officers go to some destination for three days. What was the benefit of this? The approach changed. When the British ruled over us, the officers' job was to keep the British heads happy. Today we're an independent country. Officers should not do 'sarkari' work to keep the government happy; instead, they should work for the people.)

A system must have a strong [sub] system to redress grievances. We have started a 'swagat' online portal in Gujarat. If a government officer refuses to serve a citizen the later can tell him, 'Either do the work or I will go online [to the site and file a complaint].' That's empowerment. I devote one day of every month to this. I analyse problems to find out which are due to policy, which are due to a person and which are due to a faulty process.

Modi noted that the government alone cannot do everything. He illustrated his point by giving an example, 'The Sardar Savovar dam project was started in Gujarat during Pandit Nehru's time. A canal, around 400 km, was to be made. It is still not complete. We started a fresh project which had approximately the same canal length very recently. I involved farmers of the ten districts that were to benefit. The whole thing was done in two years.'

Speeches that Demonstrate Action

Modi has emerged as a man of action who doesn't tolerate nonsense. He takes hard decisions and then sticks to them.

Enumerating a typical problem faced by men of action while implementing policies he illustrated his resolve to act despite all odds by narrating something out of the ordinary to the audience at the India Today Conclave:

> We decided to have an 'Urban Development Year' in Gujarat. If development has to progress, you need to handle encroachments. When government machinery started removing unauthorized construction there was a big hue and cry. The press gave us negative publicity. I was under pressure from my party also. I didn't realize that few months hence there were municipal elections. My party said that it would impact us negatively during elections. I told them that since now the decision has already been taken, we will not go back on our decision. Therefore we began taking action and more than Rs 900 crore worth of property had to be demolished. We got negative publicity but many said, 'At least somebody is doing something.'
>
> During this drive a lot of records were unearthed and officers discovered several big people who had not paid taxes. Usually 98 per cent pay but the big fish get away. I told my officers that if you go the legal way, you will not be able to recover money because the legal process is lengthy and these guys can afford big lawyers. The question was how to recover money from such people.

He then explained what he did.

> We did something very different. My officers went and told them that they should pay within a stipulated time frame. And if they don't pay then we will send drum beaters to their homes who would create a ruckus outside their houses every day. Their whole colony would get to know that they are defaulters. On hearing this, they all paid their taxes. There was no dispute, no need for courts.

Projecting a Vision—Generating Hope

While addressing the Indian diaspora in Berlin, Modi spoke in Hindi. Any Indian settled abroad loves to speak his own language and that is why Modi chooses to speak in Hindi whenever he addresses Indians abroad.

As if motivating the audience he said,

> *Ham log har cheez ko apne hisab se modify kar lete hain. Hamari mahilaye pizza, Chinese food aur Mexican food bhi kuch Indian tarike se bana leti hain. Ham log observe bhi accha kartey hain. Main yahan ek industrial exhibition mein gaya to unhone ek stall par mujhe technology dikhayi jo ki car ke defect ko dhoondti hai aur result screen par aa jata hai. Maine poocha kya ham ise security ke liye develop nahi kar sakte? Unhone kaha ki hamne ye kabhi soocha he nahi.'* (We [Indians] modify everything to our preferences. Our ladies even make pizzas, Chinese food and Mexican food Indian-style. We are also very observant. When I went to an industrial exhibition here they showed me a technology which finds defects in cars and displays them on a screen. I asked, 'Can we develop this technology for security purposes?' They said this idea had never occurred to them.

Reiterating his point about Make in India, he said,

> When the Industrial Revolution took place, we were slaves [to the British]. We couldn't take advantage of the revolution. When the next revolution, which was the IT revolution, happened, we put our stamp on it, because by then we were free. Our youth made India proud. Now we have to make India a manufacturing hub. If we miss this opportunity, it will be a huge loss for us.

Urging the diaspora to contribute to the nation he said, 'Our engineers are working here. You have knowledge, experience.

You have achieved all this with your hard work. Can you not build a bridge—a bridge not between two countries but one which will enable India to move forward?'

Modi is not only a good observer, he is a quick learner too. He never leaves an opportunity to learn new things. He brilliantly uses his ideas to give life to his speeches. Illustrating this, he said,

> I had gone to watch the Olympics in the US. I wanted to learn how such a big event is organized. I met students from Atlanta University. There were students from different countries at the university. I met them and tried to understand what their plans were for the future. The Chinese students were clear—they said that they would work here [in the US] for ten years and then go back to their country and use the experience gained for its benefit. All of them had this fire in them; it should be there in us as well.

He has a firm conviction that manufacturing will be India's next big thing. Our manufacturing sector's requirement is so high that other countries cannot even begin to grasp its scale.

He brilliantly illustrated the meaning and importance of value addition in a speech:

> Agri processing is an area where it is necessary to add value. For example, if we grow a mango and make pickle out of it, that is adding value. If the pickle is packaged nicely that adds more value. Then if you put a photo of a beautiful actress on the bottle that's another value-add. *Hamein technology chahiye takey sabzi paida ho, katey, pakey aur phir khai ja sakey. Yeh ham sari duniya main export kar sakte hain. Yeh hamne chai ke utpadan main karke dikhaya. Yeh ab baki cheezon main bhi karna hai.* (We need the technology to grow, process and

make vegetables ready to eat. Then we can export this all over the world. We did this in the production of tea; now we should do this for other products too.)

Talking about the tourism industry he told the Indian diaspora in Germany that they are India's brand ambassadors. He asked them to try and motivate five German families a year to visit India: '*Agar aap Bhagat Singh nahin ban sakte to kuch aur kar sakte hain.*' (If you have cannot become Bhagat Singh, you can do something else for the country). Taking the discussion on tourism one step forward he said,

> We have made one more mistake. We serve food to tourists comprising dishes that are served in Paris or America. We should serve food items that are our Indian specializations. We have such great temples and heritage buildings. In the US when I wanted to see their oldest monument they showed me the Washington Bell in Pennsylvania. Can it be compared with Ajanta–Ellora or the Suryavanshi temple which is a thousand years old?

He then asked,

> *Hamein pehle swabhiman wapas lana hoga. Hamein doosron se seekhna hoga. Main kal Berlin railway station dekne ja raha hoon. Koi pradhan mantri railway station jata hai? Main dekhne ja raha hoon ki acha station kaisa hota hai aur ham bhi aisey station banayen.* Can we become exporters and not importers? (We first need to restore our self-respect. We should learn from others. Tomorrow I am going to visit Berlin railway station. [You may wonder] Does a prime minister ever visit a railway station? But I am going to see what a good station looks like, so that we can make such stations in India.)

New Ideas, New Alliances

Modi can suggest some brilliant projects. He once mentioned how he had suggested to former Prime Minister Manmohan Singh that putting solar panels along a 1-kilometre canal could generate 1 megawatt of power. It would also save 1 crore litres of water as the water would not evaporate.

As chief minister of Gujarat, Modi, while addressing thousands of farmers from all over India at the Vibrant Gujarat Global Agricultural Summit at Gandhinagar on 9 September 2013, came up with some brilliant ideas.

> I suggested to PM Manmohan Singh that farmers around a 50-kilometre radius of big towns should grow vegetables as they have a ready market. Identify 500 towns and do the waste management in such a way that it produces organic fertilizer to be supplied to these farmers free of cost. Let them use only organic fertilizers. You will save money on the subsidy you give on chemical fertilizer and people will get organic vegetables.

He continued, 'I then gave the PM another suggestion. India should make a league of nations that are blessed with sunshine. Let us call it the Sunson Movement. India should lead this. Create a corpus for research for generating cheap solar energy. This will give the world clean energy.'

Modi can come up with some of the most brilliant and innovative ideas. He also demonstrates the ability to execute them on ground. Most importantly, he rallies political will to support his ideas. Before Modi, India lacked the political will to do something new; political leaders never demonstrated the ability to think out of the box and recycled the same old ideas for almost seven decades.

As an orator, Modi comes out as a man who infuses confidence in his audiences, a man of ideas and a man of action. Every individual sitting in the audience perceives him to be a well-meaning and genuine leader who can get things done, and that is what matters.

'Simplicity is the ultimate sophistication.'
—Leonardo da Vinci

ORATORY AND LEADERSHIP LESSONS FROM A GREAT SPEAKER

- Great speakers present actionable ideas. They address people's concerns and their problems. They are able to suggest solutions through dialogue. Such leaders have the ability to generate hope and build trust. Great orators impress their audience with their strong content, because rhetoric can only work if one has something worthwhile to say. Narendra Modi, in speech after speech, has demonstrated his ability to address problems that have plagued India for nearly seven decades. He has taken full advantage of the lack of political will, lack of political courage and lack of politically backed practical ideas, and has presented himself as a man who can do it all.
- Being absolutely clear-headed is essential. Modi, through his public dialogue, has repeatedly demonstrated that he knows what he needs to do and knows how to get it done. These are the two most important lessons for speakers who want to present their ideas convincingly in front of others.
- Out-of-the-box thinking grabs the attention of your audience. Modi impresses his audiences by coming up with solutions which others in the past could never think of. Simple yet workable ideas impress the intellect as well as ordinary minds.
- Leading by example motivates the audience. Now this is important for a speaker's creditability. You can't preach punctuality if you don't practise it yourself. Modi started from the top to set his own house in order and let people know what he was doing.
- A speaker must exhibit futuristic thinking. Modi

has demonstrated to his audience that he is always ahead of time. He shows great understanding as far as applied technology is concerned. This reflects in all his new projects and policies. His speeches clearly define a technology-based road map.
- A speaker must present a fresh perspective. Modi, on several occasions, has provided a fresh perspective on age-old problems. His idea of 'the problem of farmers is not electricity, it is water' has given a separate set of solutions to the shortage of electricity.
- Great speakers forge alliances with the audience to generate hope. A speaker has to motivate his audience through his speeches. Modi does this by generating hope. He points out to his audience that India and Indians have talent and resources and, if they decide to act, a lot can be achieved.

7

USING THE PAST TO INSPIRE THE FUTURE

History. Histrionics. Humour. Mythology. Common Sense. Culture

'Study the past if you would define the future.'
—Confucius

India thrives on its mythology, rituals, traditions, beliefs, culture and heritage. Several generations have grown up on the Ramayana and the Mahabharata. We Hindus worship Shiva, we worship Hanuman, Vishnu, avatars and deities. We believe the belief. We are proud of our Vedas and we practise inclusiveness and demonstrate tolerance. We respect heritage and our elders. We are proud of Tagore, Vivekananda, Gandhi and Subhas Chandra Bose. As one of the oldest civilizations, we also have a great legacy which we love to talk about.

Garnishing a Good Speech with History, Tradition, Culture and Mythology

Perhaps no other political leader in the history of modern India has understood this fact and connected it to his political rhetoric

USING THE PAST TO INSPIRE THE FUTURE

as innovatively as Narendra Modi. His speeches, laced with historical facts, traditions and tidbits of mythology, are compelling and captivating. He uses a commonsensical approach and illustrates his point by using simple examples which can be understood by the lowest common denominator in the audience. Modi uses these points very intelligently, sparingly, cautiously and judiciously. This gives him an instant connect with his audience and opens the flood gates to millions of hearts as though instantaneously. In every speech, where necessary, he can tuck in a simple example or two, sometimes from our Indian culture, and appears to be a man of thousand expressions.

Addressing schoolchildren on teacher's day he said,

Ham har saal sunte hain ki pichle saal se iss saal sardi zyada ho gai hai. Aisa nahi hai. Ham badal gaye hain. Hamari aadat kharab ho gai hai. Agar hame apna vatavaran bachana hao to manushya prakriti se jhagda na kare. Hamari sanskriti main ham chand ko chanda mama kehte hain. Jab ham so kar subah uthtey hain to hamari ma kehti hai, 'Bête dharti par kadam rakhne se pehle dharti se mafi mangon kyun ki tum uspar wazan daal rahe ho'. Yeh hamari sanskriti main hai. Nagpur main poornima ki raat sari streetlights band kardi jati hain. Log chandani ka maza uthate hai aur bijlee bhi bachate hai.

(Every year we get to hear that this year is colder than the last year. This is not true. We have changed, our habits have changed. If we want to save our environment we should stop fighting with nature. We call the moon 'chanda mama' [moon uncle]. When we get up in the morning and before we put our feet on the ground our mother tells us to seek forgiveness from mother earth because we are going to to put our weight on her. This is in our culture. In Nagpur on full moon night all street lights are switched off so that people can enjoy the moonlight and we save electricity also.)

Addressing Indians settled in China he talked about Indo–Chinese cooperation in managing climate change. *'Yeh museebat aadmi ne paida ki hai to mukti bhi aadmi hi dila sakta hai. Aaj se hazaron saal pehle jab pani saaf tha, ped paudhe theek the, tab bhi hamein rishi-muni kehte the prakriti se pyar karo. Poora brahmand tumhara parivar hai.'* (Man has created this problem and man has to find a solution. Thousands of years ago when there was clean water and enough greenery the sages told us that we should love nature. The whole universe is our family.)

The quotes he references from our history and tradition, about rishis' opinion on conservation of resources, especially water, create an impact on Indians in India as well as abroad.

While at Australia, Modi unveiled Gandhi's statue and said,

> Mahatma Gandhi is still very relevant, his teachings can greatly benefit the world. Ahimsa is what Gandhi preached and that is my article of faith. Gandhi said, *'Shabd se bhi hinsa na karen.' Lekin aaj hum holier than thou hain, apne ko sabse bada mante hain. Issi liye terrorism badh raha hai. Hamne prakriti ka shoshan kiya hai. Issliye global warming ho rahi hai. 1925 main Sabarmati nadi paani se poori bhari hui thi. Gandhiji tab bhi kehte the ki paani bachao. Agar aaj ham paani bachaye to global warming ko theek kiya ja sakta hai.*
>
> (Gandhi said, 'Don't commit violence even with words.' But today we are holier than thou, we think we are the most important. That is why there is so much terrorism. We have gone against nature and that is why we have global warming. Sabarmati river was full in 1925 and Gandhiji that time also asked people to save water. If we save water we can control global warming.)

Talking about the philosophy of Karma Yog, Modi said,

Main ek bar train mein safar kar raha tha. Maine ek balak ko dekha jo mushkil se chal pa raha tha, lekin wo boot polish kar raha tha train ke dabbey main. Uske pass ek Times of India *ka newspaper tha. Jab tak wo polish karta, uska grahak newpaper padhkar time guzarta tha. Yeh hi Karma Yog hai. Apna kaam achi tarah karna hi Karma Yog hai.*

(Once while I was travelling in a train, I saw a boy who could barely walk but was polishing passengers' shoes. He had a copy of the *Times of India* newspaper which he gave his clients to read while he polished the shoes. This is Karma Yog. Doing your work properly is Karma Yog.)

Addressing Indians during his Berlin visit, he inspired them by speaking about India's rich heritage. He said that we needed to be proud about our heritage.

Maine ek bar 800 saal purani moorti dekhi. Woh moorti ek pregnant aurat ki thi. Uska pet kata hua tha, aur usme bacchey ki position dikhayi gayi thi. Skin ki ek-ek layer darshayi gayi thi. Humare logon ko 800 saal pehle itna gyan tha. Humein isper garv hona chahiye.

(Once I saw an 800-year-old statue. It was of a pregnant woman. The stomach was open and child's position could be seen. Every layer of the skin was shown. Our people had so much knowledge 800 years ago. We should be proud of it.)

Talking about recycling he once said, '*Ham to ghar par bhi recycling karte hain. Jab badey bacche ka sweater chota ho jata hai to ma usko sambhal kar rakhti hai, aur wahi sweater, baad mein chotey ladke ke kaam aa jata hai.*' (We do recycle stuff even at our homes. When a sweater of the elder child becomes tight, the mother keeps it in a safe place. Later, the same sweater can be used by the younger son.)

While inaugurating a hospital in Mumbai he said, 'We can feel proud of what our country achieved in medical science at one point of time. We all read about Karna in the Mahabharata. He was not born from his mother's womb. This means genetic science was present at that time. Ganesha must have got an elephant's head with the help of plastic surgery.'

This statement was criticized by many. But one way of looking at it is that the ancient Indian civilization at least possessed a thought process and a great deal of imagination.

The Western philosophers, sci-fi writers and thinkers started fantasizing about scientific advancements only a couple of centuries ago, whereas Indians came up with such ideas thousands of years back. With this example, Narendra Modi hints at our ability to imagine the unimaginable thousands of years back as a civilization. The other civilizations started thinking in the sci-fi space much later.

For instance, Jules Verne wrote science fiction—*From the Earth to the Moon* in 1877, and *Off on a Comet* even earlier, in 1865—at a time when rocket science was not even a distant dream; these books, of course, gave encouragement to scientists.

Humour and Sarcasm

Narendra Modi is very cautious while taking a humorous dig at someone. He is sarcastically humorous and uses this ability sparingly.

For example, taking a dig at the current system of governance, where there are more laws and acts than required, he illustrated how futile rule and regulations on paper without action are by narrating an anecdote.

> *Do dost jungle main sher ka shikaar karne gaye. Woh thodi jaldi pahunch gaye to woh tehalney ke liye nikal pade. Woh gun apni*

jeep mein hi chod gaye. Woh kuch door gaye to samne se sher aa gaya. Ab gun toh thi nahin aur sher samne tha, kya karte? Unhone pocket mein se gun ka licence nikala aur sher ko dikha diya!

(Two friends went for shikar to a jungle. Since they reached early they went for a walk. They had left their gun in the jeep. After walking for a while, they encountered a lion. Since they did not have their gun they took out the gun licence and showed it to the lion!)

Addressing Parliament, he talked about the UPA government complaining about copying their ideas.

Aap kehte hain ki yeh to nayi bottle main purani sharab hai. Hamari to batein hain, sharab mein aapki baat hi aur hai. Agar yahi baat hai to aap yeh to maante hain ki jo ham kar rahe hain, woh aapko bhi pata tha.

(You say it is old wine in a new bottle. You know more about wine than we do. At least you agree that what we are doing now was known to you earlier.)

Talking about the attitude of the erstwhile UPA government he says,

Mahabharat mein Duryodhan ko kisine poocha ki tumhe such aur jhoot ki samajh hai? Duryodhan ne jawab diya, main dharma ko janta hoon, main sahi aur galat ka bhi matlab samjhta hoon. Par kya karoon, sahi kaam karna to meri fitrat main hi nahin hai. Yeh mere DNA mein hi nahin hai.

(Someone asked Duryodhan in the Mahabharata, did he know the difference between right and wrong? He said he knew the difference, but what could he do, doing the right thing was not in his DNA.)

Taking a dig at the degree of difficulty in governing a nation and how earlier governments have been ruling the country with callousness, he once told his audience, '*Ek bar ek mantriji ne apne driver se kaha ki woh us din khud gaadi chalayenge. Driver bola, mantriji yeh car hai sarkar nahin hai jo koi bhi chalale.*' (One day a minister told his driver that he would drive the car himself. The driver said that it was a car and not sarkar [government] which anybody can run.)

When asked about Sonia Gandhi's '*maut ka saudagar*' (she had referred to him as the 'angel of death') remark on a talk show, instead of getting upset he retorted that Sonia may have inadvertently used a wrong word. '*Unki matrabhasha Italian hai, uske kaaran woh shabd ko samajh nahin payi. Haqueequat mein to tha "Mat ka saudagar", woh bechari bol gayi "maut ka saudagar"* (Her mother tongue is Italian and because of that she could not understand the word. Actually it was 'Mat (vote) ka saudagar' the poor lady by mistake said 'maut ka saudagar')

Yet another of his one-liners that left an impact on the audience was when during the general election campaign he said, '*2014 ka chunao bataiyega ke kisko PM banana hai—desh bechney walon ko ya chai bechne wale ko.*' (2014 election will decide who will become the PM—those who sold the country or the person who sold tea.)

Histrionics

Whether standing on the floor of Parliament, speaking to schoolchildren or addressing an intellectually charged forum, Narendra Modi can reach out to all. People love his histrionics, his audience feels he is one of them; the man next door, a man who belongs to them.

Modi has the knack of responding obliquely and yet very effectively. In Parliament he was asked how he would ensure that Muslims would be safe in India. He responded by saying

> *Jab main Bihar mein apni rally mein bol raha tha, to wahan bomb dhamake ho rahe the, khoon ki nadiyan beh rahi thi. Maine poocha kya Hindu Musalman se ladna chahta hai, aur Musalman Hindu se, ya saab milkar gareebi se ladna chahte ho? Aaj log vikas chahte hain, log dharam jati se upar uthana chahte hai.*
>
> (When I was addressing a rally in Bihar, there were bomb blasts and there was blood everywhere. I asked whether a Hindu wanted to fight a Muslim and a Muslim a Hindu, or did they all want to come together and fight poverty? Today people want progress. People want to rise above cast and religion.)

Modi is quick on his feet to respond and is able to put across his point as a melodramatic performer. He cleverly combines criticism, history and humour and does so as smoothly as an accomplished dancer who combines Bharatnatyam with the hip hop style of dancing in a reality show. This quality of Narendra Modi makes him a fascinating speaker who enthrals audiences with every speech he delivers.

One has to acquire this quality and make constant and consistent efforts to attain perfection.

Multiple Audiences, Similar Messages

Without being repetitive, Modi knows how to use the same example from Indian history and culture differently for different audiences. While addressing 1,300 diplomats at a UNESCO meet he referred to the Clean Ganga Project as an effort in the direction of unity, saying, 'Culture must connect people and not divide them. Ganga is a part of our culture, it is a part of our religion and it is a symbol of knowledge for every Indian.'

When addressing the Indian diaspora abroad he played the emotional card by asking, 'Would you all like to bathe in Mother Ganga or not? [A] Clean and pure Mother Ganga' and drew resounding applause. Modi understands that Indians settled abroad are still very much emotionally connected with the Ganga and 'Ganga Jal', the spiritual purity associated with its waters. And therefore a positive remark about the Ganga will always invoke a positive response.

'A sense of humour…is needed armour. Joy in one's heart and some laughter on one's lips is a sign that the person down deep has a pretty good grasp of life.'
—Hugh Sidey

ORATORY AND LEADERSHIP LESSONS FROM A BRILLIANT SPEAKER

- Most civilizations thrive on their own mythology and beliefs. We all love stories and fables. When these are intelligently weaved into the content, they can make a world of difference to even an ordinary speech. Narendra Modi has mastered the art of blending Hindu-Indian culture, rituals and beliefs into his mainstream thought process.
- Modi demonstrates a great sense of understanding his audience and then pitches the same point differently in front of different target segments. He will, for instance, refer to the Ganga river in a different manner while speaking to Indians abroad than when he addresses an economic forum.
- Narendra Modi knows what the emotional arousal points of the audience are. For instance he has reached the hearts of millions of Indians by promoting yoga. Killing two birds with one stone he has also created a great image of Indian culture across the world, by launching the International Yoga Day on 21 June 2015.
- A great speaker is able to link culture and heritage to our everyday life and is able to portray it in the context that is relevant to the audience. Modi, for example, links Gandhi to global warming and the theory of karma to a boy polishing shoes for a living.
- Modi is able to link science to mythology. He can connect the Mahabharata with rocket science. A great speaker understands the audience and what is close to its 'mythological heart'. It may not be scientifically proven, but it is a belief that plays out the charm.

8

STOP ME IF YOU CAN

Packaging Ideas and Presenting Them Effectively

'Great minds discuss ideas; average minds discuss events; small minds discuss people.'
—Eleanor Roosevelt

To come up with new ideas is a mark of intelligence. However, ideas are like products—they have to be packaged and presented properly for people to buy them. Great leaders present their multiple mission statements in attractive packages and reiterate their overall vision by using these statements. Whether one makes a pitch in a corporate boardroom or participates in a college debate, the packaging of ideas matters. Yet, many orators fail to pay attention to such important aspects of oratory.

Narendra Modi has mastered the art of packaging his ideas. He presents them in a way that the lowest denominator in his audience is able to absorb these.

Modi's Pre-election Stance

While campaigning for the general elections, Modi had to

project himself as a saviour of India and at the same time hit out at the opposition without appearing too aggressive. He therefore focused on his own vision and occasionally, very carefully, pointed out the shortcomings of the UPA regime. He was being criticized by the Congress for the Godhra riots, for over-projecting his achievements and his authoritative style of governance, yet they could not provoke Modi to lose his focus.

In response to such criticism he said, 'The more mud you sling at me, the more lotuses will bloom.' With one sentence he conveyed to the audience that criticism by the opposition didn't bother him and in a way helped him.

Time and again he reminded the voters that India needed a stable and strong government. A fractured mandate leading to a coalition government would be a disaster for democracy. This fact had to be hammered into the minds of voters across a country as geographically vast as India, with an electorate as huge as 125 crore. Yet Modi expressed his concern in the most positive way by saying, 'Give me a stable government, I will give you a strong India.' He promised a people-friendly government with an appeal of 'Pro-people good governance'.

He explained the economic potential of India with his idea of the three Ds—Democracy, Demography and Demand.

Wooing the World for Destination India

Modi understood the fact that India would need massive investment for his vision to take off and said so, on 25 September 2014 at the launch of the 'Make in India' global initiative. His idea of 'think East, link West' sent a strong signal to the international community, urging them to understand that both the East and the West needed to work together.

Foreign direct investment (FDI) was the need of the hour and Modi was all for it. Yet, he emphasized development as the fundamental tenet of foreign investment when he said, 'First develop India then foreign direct investment.' For his dream, 'Make in India' he says, 'Sell anywhere, but manufacture here.'

Committing to Commitment

Modi has demonstrated that he is a powerhouse of human energy and he is willing to spend every ounce of that energy to take India to greater heights. 'In my life, mission is everything. Even if I was a municipal chairman, I would have worked as hard as a chief minister' is the way he describes his workaholic nature. He often says, 'Hard work never brings fatigue. It brings satisfaction.' His mantra for success is simple and straightforward.

'Desire + Strategy = Resolution
Resolution + Hardwork = Success'

Modi has been urging the masses to work collectively towards nation-building. '*Agar har Bharatwasi ek kadam agey badhayega to desh 125 crore kadam agey badhega.*' (If every Indian citizen takes one step forward, the nation moves 125 crore steps ahead.) He once said, 'The mind is never a problem, the mindset is. We have to change our mindset.' From the ramparts of the Red Fort, addressing the nation for the first time as prime minister, he said, '*Nirasha ka mahol bana hua hai. Lekin democracy ki strength aisi hai ki ek garib admi aaj aapke samne khara hai.*' (There is an atmosphere of gloom. But the strength of democracy is such that a poor man is standing in front of you.)

He said, '*Humein aapni soch badalni hai. Hum jab kam karen to yeh na sochein ki isme mera kya, mujhe kya?*' (We need to change our thinking. When we do any work we should not think of what [profit] is there in it for us.)

He believes that the government cannot do everything. Governments can have good policies, build some infrastructure but the country can progress only with the participation of the people. He believes that Mahatma Gandhi was successful because he made the fight for freedom into a People's Revolution. For his Swachh Bharat campaign, referencing Mahatma Gandhi, he said, '*Mahatma Gandhi ne satyagraha shuroo kiya, humein aab swachtagraha shuru karna hai.*' (Mahatma Gandhi started satyagraha; we need to start swachtagraha.)

To help the poor, and thus help the country progress, he urged the rich to give up their LPG gas cylinder subsidy so that more gas connections could be provided to the poorer people, saying, '*Jo aadmi hotel mein rehne ke liye 20,000 rupaye deta hai, usko LPG subsidy chahiye kya? Subsidy se paka khaana shobha deta hai kya?*' (A person who spends Rs 20,000 to stay in a hotel, does he need LPG subsidy? For such people eating food cooked on subsidized gas doesn't look good.)

During his election campaign, Modi projected himself not only as a hard-working and committed leader, but also as an honest one. The previous UPA government had been rocked by several scams and Modi mounted scathing attacks in this regard.

'*Jinhone gandgi karni thi, woh kar gaye. Hum ab saaf karenge* (Those who had to create filth have done it, we will clean it now),' he said while addressing the Indian diaspora in Toronto. He went on to say, '*Na mein khaoonga, na khane doonga*' (Neither will I take a bribe nor will I allow anyone to take one) and '*Hume scam India se skill India banana hai*' (From scam India we have to make skill India).

Modi has a knack of presenting himself to the opposition

in the most humble way, when required. In his first address to the Rajya Sabha he said, '*Main bahut naya hoon, meri raksha karna*' (I am very new, please protect me). This way he disarmed the opposition parties who were otherwise ready to attack him.

Ability to Criticize Appropriately

On several occasions Modi has been criticized for being very high-handed and arrogant. To this he once responded,

> *Yeh [Congress members] arrogance ki baat karte hain. 1982 mein jab Rajiv Gandhi Congress ke general secretary the aur unhe Andhra Pradesh ke Chief Minister T. Anjaiah Hyderabad ke Begumpet airport par receive karne aaye to Rajiv Gandhi ne sabke saamne unki bezati kar di. Is baat se Shri Anjaiah bahut upset ho gaye. Aur us samaye Rajiv Gandhi koi government position par nahin the.*

> (They [Congress members] talk about arrogance. In 1982 when Rajiv Gandhi was general secretary of the Congress, the then CM of Andhra Pradesh T. Anjaiah received him at Hyderabad's Begumpet airport and Rajiv Gandhi insulted him publicly. Anjaiah was very upset by this. Moreover at that time Rajiv Gandhi held no government position.)

Modi has mastered the art of creating slogans and witty statements, and hitting the right emotional notes intelligently and very quickly. He can create appropriate expressions for his audience with ease. He delivers a measured response to criticism and rarely goes overboard while criticizing opponents, even if they try to provoke him.

'The world is looking at Asia. I don't have to waste time in inviting people. I need to give them the address.'
—Narendra Modi

ORATORY AND LEADERSHIP LESSONS FROM A BRILLIANT SPEAKER

- Packaging and presenting ideas is an art essential for good public speaking. Ideas are like products and unless they are packaged well, the audience will not buy them.
- Narendra Modi presented himself as a saviour of India; he projected himself as a symbol of hope for the people, who were disillusioned with the political system and the way they were governed for the last few decades.
- A speaker must build a perception in the minds of people. Modi did two things—first he presented himself as a powerhouse of energy and a man who could turn things around; second, he convinced his countrymen that change was possible and simultaneously wooed foreign investors by telling them that India had changed and it was a great opportunity for them to invest.
- Modi built a positive vibe and created goodwill using meaningful slogans like 'All together, all grow' and about bribes, 'I won't hog, and I won't allow hogging.' He promised to work for the people and create a government which would work for the people by coining an acronym, P2G2—Pro-People Good Governance.
- For his dream of making India a manufacturing hub, he coined a slogan, 'Make in India' and a supportive argument, 'Sell anywhere but manufacture here.'
- Leaders learn to take criticism in their stride. It is very important not to react to provocations. Modi does criticize his opponents but his response has always been measured and infrequent.

9

FIRST AMONGST EQUALS

Creating a Unique Lexicon

'No poet or orator has ever existed who believed there was any better than himself.'
—Marcus Tullius Cicero

To make a distinct place for himself in a political party which has produced orators of the calibre of Atal Bihari Vajpayee, Arun Jaitely and Sushma Swaraj, Narendra Modi had to be nothing short of extraordinarily brilliant. In order to match up to these seasoned stalwarts who had proven themselves at the national level, on the floor of Parliament and in numerous campaigns for decades, he had to be different. Today Narendra Modi not only stands head and shoulders above speakers on the home turf but also stands like a rock star amongst greats like Winston Churchill, John F. Kennedy, Barack Obama, Martin Luther King, Douglas MacArthur, Franklin D. Roosevelt, Fidel Castro, Golda Meir, Charles de Gaulle and Mikhail Gorbachev.

Each one of these speakers has been able to mesmerize the audience and leave a lasting impact on history. Therefore, to compare one with the other would be unfair to them, as well as to the art of oratory and public speaking. Yet, each one of them had a distinct style and was able to create a unique lexicon and an impact for the world to see.

Parables and stories have been used by almost all the great speakers of the world because they are the most effective way to capture the attention of the audience. Even Jesus Christ used parables to illustrate some profound truths, using symbols from daily life—such as sheep, bread, and salt—as such parables were easily understandable and people could relate to them; stories such as these are easily retained because they use bold characters and symbolisms which have rich meaning.

Modi uses anecdotes, parables and mythology very effectively in his speeches, while steering clear of touching upon the topic of religion because of its sensitive nature. This is one aspect of public speaking which is very important and must be kept in mind by all those who address large heterogeneous audiences.

Narendra Modi possesses almost all the qualities that great speakers have. Yet he has created his own unique style, his own lexicon and a skill that most would envy. Before a live telecast, a radio chat show or a speech given on stage, Modi's audiences always expect something fresh, something new, something innovative and he never disappoints them.

He has left an indelible mark on his audiences, whether speaking in India or during his whirlwind tours abroad. It would be worthwhile to compare Modi's style with others, past and present, who have been able to achieve similar results. Such an analysis will help the reader understand the unique methods and craft employed by the world's greatest speakers.

Atal Bihari Vajpayee

Atal Bihari Vajpayee, the former prime minister of India, called 'Gentle Giant' by Arun Jaitely, played beautifully with words to impress his audience but was always measured. He had a way with words and was as great a wordsmith as Winston Churchill. Very few political leaders have used poetry with prose as elegantly as Vajpayee, who created brilliant speeches that left audiences enthralled. He spoke slowly and emphatically, and combined his acting and theatrical skills to make a lasting impact. He commanded a huge stage presence, and generously mixed humour and sarcasm with substance to reach out to his audiences.

Vajpayee had the advantage of a rich vocabulary and could speak extempore on practically any subject. He spoke spontaneously, thinking on his feet, yet managing to respond appropriately even on the floor of Parliament.

Once, politician and opposition MP Ram Vilas Paswan quipped that the BJP talked about Ram and Ram Mandir, though there was nobody called Ram in the BJP, though there was Ram in Ram Vilas Paswan. Vajpayee retorted in Hindi, 'Paswan ji, the word 'haram'[forbidden/banned/taboo] also has 'ram' in it!' That's how quick-witted he was.

Narendra Modi, on the other hand, is neither poetic nor philosophical, but is very direct. His style and substance are such that he seems to conspire with the audience almost all the time. He speaks for his audience, and it is 'us' and not 'I' in his speeches, much like Barack Obama. His sartorial style—colourful kurtas and matching Modi jackets with appropriate footwear—presents the appearance of one who is fully in control and is powerfully impeccable.

Modi's greatest asset is that he speaks without referring to notes and tailors his speeches to suit the audience. He uses political rhetoric at rallies, means business at investors' meets, and shows wisdom on the floor of Parliament. He mostly speaks in the language he is comfortable with—Hindi.

Modi emphasizes words that matter, which makes his speeches retentive. He does not use difficult words at all, though he sometimes uses Sanskrit shlokas for impact. This is something worth appreciating—that bombastic words alone don't make an impact. In fact, simpler the narrative, the better it is.

Mark Twain once narrated a tale about a Missouri farmer who used very big and difficult words and lost five state legislative elections. One day, when he was as usual practising his speeches while milking his cows, he was kicked in the face by a cow, knocking his front teeth out. That left him able to only speak words of one syllable and he won his next election, noted Twain. The moral of the story is that leaders who get their point across simply are usually more successful in winning over an electorate.

Winston Churchill

One of the most celebrated British prime ministers and one of the world's greatest modern orators, Churchill had a vast vocabulary because he was a voracious reader. Where an average person would have 25,000 words in his vocabulary, Churchill was estimated as having 65,000. As Maurice Druon said, 'I love English. I learnt it from the speeches of Winston Churchill.'

Churchill also had a great memory, as Modi has. He carried a huge database of anecdotes in his head and easily pulled out the right anecdote at the right time. And, like Modi, Churchill's speeches could create images in the minds of his audience. For instance, his speech on the floor of Parliament on 4 June 1940, popularly referred to as 'We will fight them on the beaches...' is one of the most monumental speeches. An excerpt is reproduced below:

> We shall go on to the end, we shall fight in France, we shall fight on the seas and oceans, we shall fight with growing confidence and growing strength in the air, we shall defend our Island, whatever the cost may be, we shall fight on the beaches, we shall fight on the landing grounds, we shall fight in the fields and in the streets, we shall fight in the hills; we shall never surrender, and even if, which I do not for a moment believe, this Island or a large part of it were subjugated and starving, then our Empire beyond the seas, armed and guarded by the British Fleet, would carry on the struggle, until, in God's good time, the New World, with all its power and might, steps forth to the rescue and the liberation of the old.

Churchill's language was conversational, though very rich and beautiful—here he could be better compared to Vajpayee than Modi—and he was bestowed with a deep baritone, lending his speeches additional gravitas. Modi, too, has a powerful voice.

Abraham Lincoln

Lincoln used logic and not rhetoric to win the hearts of his audience. He was brilliant in articulation and had the ability of making himself clearly understood. He was a serious man and he appeared sad, but when he warmed up, all the sadness disappeared.

Lincoln was a thinker-philosopher who had strong views which were articulated in carefully chosen words. He was always truthful, sincere, careful, and never dictatorial or insulting. He did not gesticulate for stage effect and used his hands sparingly while he spoke.

It is said he used to think out his speeches while he went for walks. He wrote his speeches in parts and later assembled them, jotting down all the parts once again to produce the final draft, which appeared perfect when he delivered it in front of his audience. His speeches were powerful because of their strong compelling content and not because of the way he spoke.

Like Lincoln, Modi's speeches to have powerful content, and he too articulates his ideas beautifully. In addition, Modi also has great stage presence and thus delivers great impactful speeches.

Lincoln was also known to have tremendous powers of persuasion, which few have. He could hold his audience for hours together; his arguments were so persuasive and disarming that they were almost unchallengeable. Reporting on a speech he gave, a reporter of the *Chicago (Illinois) Press & Tribune* wrote on 15 October 1858, 'Of his speech, I will say that it lasted three hours and that during all the time the whole audience seemed perfectly wrapt in attention and that in power, pathos and eloquence, I have never heard it equalled.'

Narendra Modi can also go on for hours without boring his audience. In trademark fashion, he seeks more time from the audience by looking at his wristwatch, and every time his audience would rather not let him go and clamours for more.

Dwight D. Eisenhower

American President Dwight D. Eisenhower and many great speakers focused on the result they sought from the speech, in other words, its purpose, or what exactly was to be conveyed to the audience. Once they identified this, they used it as the central read to string together the speech. Eisenhower is known to have asked speech writers what the QED (quod erat demonstrandum, or that which was to be proved, or the purpose) of the speech was.

In contrast, Modi conveys several points in a speech, and using several such 'threads' weaves a complete fabric rather than sticking to a single thread.

Barack Obama

Obama gauges what his audience is thinking and accordingly goes with the flow. To keep things simple, he uses pauses and looks relaxed, calm and assertive. He relies on clear diction and inflection, chewing on every word that he utters. Like Modi, Obama uses gestures and eye contact to create the feeling of a one-on-one conversation with every individual in the audience. He places his hand over the heart to show commitment, finger pinched to demonstrate resolve, or an outstretched hand to make a point.

Obama believes in the dictum of the 'first 180 seconds' and therefore starts strong with an anecdote or a quote to catch the attention of his audience. Modi normally starts slowly but within a short time builds up the momentum. This depends on the audience. While addressing Parliament he starts slowly, as if cautiously, whereas while addressing the Indian diaspora, he often starts with an impactful dialogue.

Like Modi, Barack Obama too refers to his humble background wherever appropriate. Obama, before criticizing the opposition, first affirms its service to the nation; this helps him avoid the image of being a mudslinger. Modi also shows due respect to the opponent before criticizing, though while criticizing he doesn't spare the rod. Both Modi and Obama have been able to successfully build the impression that they can be trusted and they will be able to usher in change. Like Modi, Obama also refers to the truths in the great books such as the Bible, and shares dreams and historical facts to connect with his audience.

One striking quality which both Obama and Modi have in common is that they both come across as authentic, genuine and well-meaning leaders in every speech that they deliver. To cite just one instance, where Obama says, 'There is not a Liberal America and a Conservative America. There's United States of America,' to convey that he does not believe in the old type of politicking, Modi says, 'Our decisions are guided by rashtraneeti (national interest) and not rajneeti (politics).'

Obama, in common with Churchill, believes that the attention of the audience must be captured at the beginning of a speech. Incidentally, Churchill never praised anyone at the beginning of his speech, which he thought would be misconstrued by the audience as flattery, and therefore usually positioned praise and humour in the middle.

Modi, on the contrary, doesn't follow any such norm. 'The secret of humour is surprise,' said Aristotle; and Modi appears to follow this advice given by the master of rhetoric. He weaves humour in very cleverly, even while speaking about a serious issue.

Great speakers like Franklin D. Roosevelt and Churchill used to read their speeches out to a large extent. Modi stands tall amongst his equals in this regard, as he very rarely has a written speech in front of him.

Without doubt Modi stands tall as an orator par excellence, never witnessed before in India's contemporary history.

ORATORY AND LEADERSHIP LESSONS FROM A BRILLIANT SPEAKER

- The world's greatest speakers have been able to build a solid reputation and earned respect from their audiences due to their oratorical skills. Each one of them developed a unique style and presented himself in an extraordinary manner.
- Almost all effective speakers have learnt how to judiciously mix philosophy and facts with humour and sarcasm. Most have had a razor-sharp memory, demonstrated good command over the language and been possessed of a sound vocabulary.
- High-quality public speaking is backed by hours of preparation and hard work. The world's greatest speakers spend a considerable amount of time and invest a lot of effort in preparing their speeches. Yet they demonstrate mental agility and the ability to think on their feet.
- Very few speakers have the gift of speaking without referring to notes. Several effective speakers do use notes and follow a written script, yet they refer to their notes only on few occasions and rather sparingly. This is one skill which every speaker must try to develop.
- It is not necessary to use big and difficult words to make an impactful speech—the simpler the better. It is more important to fine-tune the content according to the audience, rather than selecting complex expressions and difficult words.
- Modi has broken the language barrier and chooses to speak in Hindi, a language he is most comfortable with. A good speech can be delivered in any language; therefore, it is not necessary to

speak to your audience only in English, a delusion many public speakers in India appear to have.
- Effective speakers use criticism and sarcasm very carefully. Usually, they first praise the opponent and only then convey their displeasure or criticism.
- The first 180 seconds are important for a speaker to establish himself on the stage. Many like Obama and Churchill broke the ice within the first three minutes. Thereafter it becomes easier to keep the audience with you for the rest of the time.
- The secret of humour is surprise. Therefore, mixing humour with serious substance appropriately is the essence of great oratory.

10

THE POWER OF THE SPOKEN WORD

The Art of Influencing People

'Nothing is so unbelievable that oratory cannot make it acceptable.'
—Marcus Tullius Cicero

Great speeches have influenced people, swayed the outcome of historical events, motivated people to wage wars, urged people to fight injustice and to even lay down their lives. Words, in other words, can comfort people during a tragedy, can move soldiers and partisans to risk life and limb, raise levels of patriotism and even change the course of history.

Oratory is thus the art of influencing people, and those who master this skill command an almost God-like power. The power of the spoken word was realized centuries ago. Great wordsmiths like Pericles, who lived nearly 2,500 years ago, beautifully demonstrated the power of eloquence. Pericles himself was acknowledged as the most prominent Greek statesman of his time, today called the Golden Age of Greece. Yet another great orator who came after him was Demosthenes, remembered as the greatest orator of all time.

Mastering the art of oratory was considered essential in ancient Greece, for those who wished to become well-rounded individuals. Oratory became central to public life because it was the essential tool for politicians to navigate through democratic government; it was essential to argue a case in a court of law. Debates and discussions, therefore, were a hallmark of this golden age of eloquence. During the same era, Roman philosophers and orators like Marcus Tullius Cicero made their mark on commoners and emperors alike. Subsequently emperors, noblemen and advisors kept this art alive and used it to their advantage throughout history.

Examining the last hundred years of contemporary history closely, marked as the period was by two World Wars, one still finds oratory at the helm of affairs. If great events create great leaders, then great events also throw up powerful speakers. Winston Churchill, Franklin D. Roosevelt or Charles de Gaulle came on the scene as great orators because of the events that caused the Second World War or because of the events triggered by the First World War. In the second half of the twentieth century the world saw people like John F. Kennedy, Ronald Reagan, Fidel Castro, Martin Luther King and Nelson Mandela as great influencers of their times.

Public Speaking vs Oratory

'In making a speech, one must study three points: first, the means of producing persuasion; second, the style or language; third, the proper arrangements of the various parts of the speech.'

—Aristotle

Webster's Dictionary defines oratory as the 'art of speaking elegantly and effectively that is characterized by use of appeals chiefly to emotions'. In contrast, the definition of public speaking does not include a reference to elegant emotional appeals. And that, in fact, is the basic difference.

While public speaking focuses on just conveying your point clearly and concisely, oratory is more persuasive and is crafted to influence the audience. It is argumentative and addresses the emotional aspect of the context. It reaches more to the heart than the head. Therefore, all oratory is public speaking but all the public speaking is not oratory.

Technically speaking there are two types of speakers, those who use reasoning and those who speak from the heart. They also reach out to two different types of audiences—those who understand through reasoned logic and those who understand and accept through the heart. Those who speak from the heart speak to people; those who speak with reason speak in boardrooms, conferences and parliaments.

Reasoning requires rationale, statistics, facts and figures to present cold logic. A person who reasons draws conclusions that cannot be easily refuted or challenged. Such discourses are academic in nature. Those who speak from their heart may also use reasoning, but only to augment their power of influence.

Great orators mix the two genres very skilfully. That is how they move on to become orators from being mere public speakers. They are master craftspersons of logic and rhetoric. Such great masters combine clear speech with simple arguments, using their instincts to say the right things at the right place to the right people, and the right number of times. Their ideas blend perfectly with their words and emotions. Such men and women understand the hidden aspirations of their audiences. Their discourses are masterpieces. In a way such orators are like chameleons, they know when and how to speak from the heart and cleverly shift back to precise logic when needed.

Remember, great speakers who connect with their audience are not only reporters or messengers, but interpreters and analysts who can make people see things in the larger context. They achieve this by reaching out to both the heads and the hearts of their audience.

Oratory encompasses all other disciplines and therefore qualifies as the highest art. It is a clever amalgam of literature, knowledge, content, prose, drama, stagecraft and even rhythm. If public speaking is a story then oratory is the story rolled out as a screenplay—sound, camera, action. It appeals to the deeper sentiments, stirs passion and arouses the audience to act according to the narrative.

Oratory can best be employed during a crisis, during times of low public morale or even during a struggle. It can be used effectively to influence business deals, seal treaties between nations or influence masses to act.

Leaders, Managers and Orators

The art of persuasion and the ability to influence and convince others is most important for success. These skills are extremely important at higher levels of leadership. For instance, an engineer remains an engineer for the first few years of his career and quickly and automatically transcends into a managerial role because he then has to manage projects, people, timelines, finance and resources. He becomes a leader who has to be heard at meetings, has to convince the bosses, buy-in the clients and motivate the team.

To convince others he needs to communicate effectively. If

he is able to understand the power of oratory and make genuine efforts to become an effective orator, he can move mountains within the context of his role.

Are Orators Born or Made?

Is oratory learnable? Can you acquire it or are you born with it? There are people who have a gift of the gab and are natural speakers. Yet there are plenty who have made efforts to become influencing personalities.

Those who are gifted have the basic ability to argue and explain their point of view, and can express their ideas in a logical way. Some are also gifted with enthusiasm and a high energy level. Such people also have strong opinions.

Modi, for instance, had the ability to explain his point of view clearly and precisely right from childhood. He also formed his own opinions and views and had the confidence to speak in front of anyone. Once he entered the political arena he gradually refined his oratorial skills, worked on his ideas and delivered them as great speeches.

Winston Churchill, on the contrary, as a newly elected member of the House of Commons at the young age of twenty-nine, got up to speak for the first time and literally froze for almost three minutes, then uttered a few words and sat down in disgust. At that point, he vowed that this would never happen again. He spent years refining, rehearsing and re-refining his speeches. He spent a lot of time in selecting the right words and the right phrases for the right context. He looked for more impactful words. He delivered hundreds of speeches and made conscious efforts to improve every performance. Thirty-six years after that first fateful speech, he became the prime minister of

England at the age of sixty-five and he had by then mastered the art of oratory. He was not a natural speaker but had mastered the craft of oratory with practice and preparation.

Steve Jobs would get nervous in front of the camera at the beginning of his career, and was edgy and nervous during several of his speeches. He could be seen clutching the lectern and often looking at his notes while he spoke. Gradually, with practice, he emerged as an effective speaker. Whether gifted or not, you can make efforts and become a great orator.

How to Become a Great Orator

If oratory is an art which can be acquired and gradually perfected, what are the basic skills that one needs to focus upon? Simply put, good oratory boils down to understanding what to say, how to speak and how to articulate your presentation.

What to say

Now this is where most people go wrong. You may have a great voice, a very high level of confidence, your body language may be fine and you may be speaking from the heart—but if your content isn't relevant and solid, you will be a disaster. You should research your facts and figures and do enough homework while preparing your speech.

Read and research: Never take a shortcut with regard to this. Prepare your speech well. You must read all relevant material and cross-check facts before you finalize your draft. Make it a habit to write down your script. If not the entire speech, at least jot down the major points you plan to make as well as what you plan to say under each point.

Cater to the audience: Keep the context in mind while developing content. Who is your audience? Whom are you addressing? What is the occasion? What exactly do you want to convey and achieve? These are some of the questions you must answer before you decide on the content. For instance, if you are addressing a women's forum, your content would be very different from a speech you might give to college students on the same topic.

Use metaphors, quotes, analogies and similes: This is extremely potent stuff that can augment your content to a great extent. Quotes by great people are available on almost every subject. The art lies in picking up the right ones for your content. Metaphors and similes act as a bridge between your ideas and your audience. Metaphors can effectively convey some very complex issues in a simple and straightforward way.

Be a storyteller: 'All human beings have an innate need to hear and tell stories and to have a story to live by... Religion, whatever else it has done, has provided one of the main ways of meeting this abiding need,' said Harvey Cox. Everyone wants to listen to a story. There is a child in everyone. An abstract or a story-based example, or a portion from history or mythology can be a very effective way of enhancing your content. People listen to these stories in rapt attention.

Mix styles and borrow ideas: Shah Rukh Khan once said in an interview that he could pick up styles from great actors of the past and portray them in his own way, in his own style, making it look original—and that is what ingenuity is.

Speak from the heart: This is easier said than done. The speaker must be convinced about the topic, only then can he speak from the heart. When you speak from your heart, you appear genuine and you connect straightaway with your audience. Your appeal must sound genuine and that can happen only if you imbue it with emotion.

Define the purpose of the speech: A speaker must be clear regarding the purpose of the speech from the very onset. And he must stick to this core purpose throughout his speech. A good orator keeps his focus on the result that he needs to achieve. Quotes, audio, video clips and humour should be used intelligently. Without humour a speech can become dry, boring and monotonous. Light humour at an appropriate moment can be very refreshing for the audience. Use clean humour; never have a laugh at anyone's cost. Also, don't insert quotes or clips that are out of context. Also, make sure these do not distract the audience or inadvertently shift the focus of the speech.

Be articulate: Put your thoughts across logically and systematically so that your speech has a definitive smooth flow. One topic should systematically lead to the next. As far as possible a speaker should never jump from topic to topic in a manner that sounds abrupt. This confuses the audience and may very well throw you off-track too. So identify the main highlights of your speech and then connect them to achieve a proper flow.

Use facts and figures: These make your speech effective and authentic. Ensure that you do not quote figures that could be challenged or may be wrong; triple-check your facts beforehand. Facts and figures at your fingertips can earn you a lot of respect.

How to speak

This aspect of oratory deals with the way a person speaks—diction (how correctly and clearly each word is word is pronounced), the modulation of voice, body language etc. It is all about theatrics—how you make an impact and how you present yourself. To achieve this you need to do the following.

Practise as much as you can: This is most essential. The more you rehearse the better you get. Write down your script, memorize the points and practise in front of a mirror, again and again and again.

Building confidence: If you are well-rehearsed, you will automatically become confident. Your first public address may be a little shaky, you may be a little apprehensive and nervous. But this is quite natural. Don't worry about failure, as failure takes you towards success.

Watch your own recordings : Use your mobile phone or any other means to record your rehearsals and even your public speaking assignments. When you watch your performance you will understand your shortcomings. Try to keep all your recordings intact and track your progress after each presentation—note three weak points and three strong points. Work on your weak points to ensure that you do not repeat your mistakes and retain your strengths.

Voice modulation: Do not speak in one tone as it becomes monotonous—a change in frequency or pitch while speaking keeps the audience alert and receptive. Be audible enough for your audience in the last row to be able to hear you; if they cannot hear you, adjust your mike. Remember, a lower pitch sounds better; avoid sounding shrill as far as possible. Moderate your volume in case you are speaking loudly. And finally, speak each word clearly; do not mumble.

Watch your pace: Audiences are usually comfortable with a person who speaks at around 125 words per minute. Therefore, keep your range between 110 to 140 words per minute. Some people speak very fast and the audience cannot grasp what they are saying. On the other hand, speaking very slowly can put the audience to sleep and make your discourse very boring.

Say the same thing in hundred different ways: Now this is not easy. A good orator can explain the same point in several different ways. And this is a superb art worth acquiring. An orator is the teacher and the audience his students. A great orator can also say the same thing to different audiences in different ways. When he addresses schoolchildren he uses one example and when addressing senior officers from the corporate world he uses a different example to convey the same point. The greatest orator can say the same thing to the same segment of the audience differently.

Avoid using a crutch/prop: Ever seen great speakers like Obama, Modi, Fidel Castro or Opera Winfrey use a PowerPoint? They speak from the heart as much as from memorized text. They speak into the mike and look into the camera. They also don't use too much audio-visual input. Yet they have changed history and motivated millions. With regard to oratory, a simple axiom says it all: if you need to use PowerPoint, then there is no power in your point!

The power of a pause: A pause can be used in two ways. Whenever there is applause or the audience laughs at a joke, the speaker must pause and wait for the applause or laughter to finish. A speaker can also use a pause very effectively to emphasize a point. Indian veteran actor Dilip Kumar said an interview that he gradually learnt the power of 'silence' during his acting career. When to keep quiet for a very short period between two sentences was an art he developed very effectively. This way you can synchronize the expectations of your audience with your speech and thought. It also makes the audience more attentive. This has to be done deliberately, intelligently and only at a few critical points of the discourse.

Listen to the radio and watch TV: Listen to good radio channels to see how different anchors, debaters and panelists speak. Observe their different styles, their punctuation pauses, their clarity of thought, their diction and pronunciation. Good TV channels select their presenters and newsreaders very carefully. Therefore, they speak and pronounce not only appropriately but also correctly.

Participate in debates: If you can find a partner to debate with, practise with them. Take the initiative and participate in school or college debates. When you are able to effectively argue in real time it will give you a tremendous boost of confidence. You cannot carry a written speech onto a debate podium and have to respond on the spot; so practising with a good debating partner will improve your skills in speaking extempore.

The fine art of stagecraft and drama: How many of us examine the podium a day before we speak? Very few. Great and effective speakers study a venue for its acoustics, colour scheme, the best places to speak from, entrances and exits, the door and windows. They learn the art of keeping their audience charged. They spring surprises appropriately.

Leadership fails when leaders sympathize rather than empathize. Sympathy is, 'I know how you feel,' while empathy is, 'I feel how you feel.' Good speakers use rhetoric to convince the audience that they empathize and not sympathize with them.

Handle unexpected issues smoothly: You may have rehearsed well and you may be very confident but unexpected problems can pop up while you are speaking in front of the audience. For instance, there could be a sudden power breakdown. Don't panic. If the power returns quickly, resume from where you left off. If it looks like it is going to take longer, then you can even declare a break. The bottom line is that you must remain cool during any such mishap.

Importance of Reading

One of the most effective methods of becoming a good orator is by acquiring knowledge and appreciating different styles of expression. You can achieve both these by reading different authors and experimenting with different subjects. Narendra Modi, is an avid reader and loves to read during his spare time, having developed the habit during his schooldays.

Reading books by many authors: Reading books by different authors exposes us to different writing styles and methods adopted by people of intellect.

Reading books from many genres: Reading books belonging to several different genres broadens our horizons, keeps us updated and eventually builds intellect. Such books arm us with facts and figures which add to our content.

Reading fiction: This is particularly important, as it lets us imagine and enhances our mental faculties. As one develops a taste for reading, one can go in for reading a bit of philosophy and history as well.

Reading the newspaper: This habit updates us on the latest trends and news. Newspapers are also very effective in terms of building content in the realm of current affairs. If one can focus on the editorials, they provide a rich resource for appreciating ideas and opinions of those who matter in the society.

Reading magazines: These are also a great source of information. They usually carry more detailed and researched articles as compared to newspapers in general.

Accessing the Internet: Today there is no dearth of reading material, and the Internet, if used intelligently, can be a 'seamless library'. It has information on every subject that you can possibly think of. Today we should consider ourselves lucky because we live in the information age and all of it is available at the click of a mouse.

One must read and try to retain as much as possible. Information in books, magazines, newspapers or on the Internet is of no use to you if you cannot keep some of it in your head and use it appropriately. Because what you have absorbed will come in handy while building your oratory skills.

Rhetoric and the Art of Persuasion

Through the centuries, going back 2,500 years, people in power have employed rhetoric very effectively. Greek and Roman scholars and orators clubbed philosophy, eloquence and oratory into one discipline of learning.

Aristotle defined rhetoric as, 'The faculty of observing in any given case the available means of persuasion.' He was of the opinion that there were three ways to persuade and convince people: (i) the speaker's own character; (ii) by appealing to the public's emotions; and, (iii) by proving to them that you are telling the truth. Some philosophers were convinced that all methods of aggressive persuasion, such as rhetoric, were lies designed to trick the audience. Therefore, sometimes people view rhetoric in a negative light.

If I were to put oratory and influence—because one is useless without other—into three words, they would be (i) style; (ii) substance; and (iii) impact. The greatest speakers of the world who could influence and motivate people had all three. As every orator is unable to study philosophy, oratory has since lost some of its substance. When oratory is separated from philosophy it tends to become empty rhetoric.

The prime objective of a good orator is to persuade his audience about specific ideas and in specific situations. What good is public speaking if the speaker cannot convince people? Rhetoric is an art, which enhances the ability of writers, more so of speakers, to motivate and persuade the audience. Speakers who do not distort facts can employ rhetoric very effectively without damaging their reputation.

Eloquence, oratory and rhetoric are very important today, because the audience is better informed in the information age and its reactions are unpredictable, arbitrary and unforeseeable.

The five canons of rhetoric

Invention: The art of finding the right argument—well-researched content as applicable to a situation.

Arrangement: This has to do with articulation, structure and sequencing of the argument. It determines the flow of speech.

Style: This is more to do with selecting the right words, forming the right sentences and using appropriate vocabulary.

Memory: How to memorize your speech, and how to use as little help as possible from notes or other devices.

Delivery: This component of rhetoric deals with body language, voice management and gestures. Cicero said, 'Without this sole and supreme power, a speaker of the highest mental capacity can be held in no esteem. One with moderate abilities, with this qualification, may surpass even that of the highest talent.'

In closing, I can quote no one better than George J. Thompson to summarize this discussion: 'The goal of persuasion is to generate voluntary compliance... The great communicators have that art. They somehow get people to do what they want them to do by getting them to want to do it... What options are available to generating voluntary compliance? The first, surprisingly enough, is your mere presence: the way you show up, the way you approach, carry yourself, stand around, even the way you project your feelings onto your face.'

Types of Speakers

Celebrity speakers

These are speakers who are highly paid, but not for their style, substance or impact. Many are paid either because of having a celebrity tag, or having been in the eye of the storm for something big. Their experience and position sells them.

If we were to examine some of the highly paid speakers of

the world, Donald Trump is said to have charged $1.5 million for a one-hour speech and Ronald Reagan $1 million for every appearance. Retired US Presidents like Bill Clinton are paid a large fee because they can share their experiences as former presidents of America. Al Gore, a former US vice-president, was famous for his crusade against global warming and hence a sought-after speaker. Former British Premier Tony Blair, and former Governor of Alaska Sarah Palin are also celebrity speakers.

Bill Gates and Richard Branson are business tycoons first and then speakers. Steven Covey and Deepak Chopra influenced people with their books first and then were called to speak and became sought-after celebrity authors.

Most celebrity speakers have a good oratory style, but have not achieved their celebrity status because of being orators. It has been the other way round—they became speakers because of their other professional achievements.

Philosophical speakers who sell ideas, substance and dreams

These are people who have become cult figures because their ideas were radically different. They had a lot of 'substance' and a philosophy which appeared to the people.

Bhagwan Rajneesh, popularly known as Osho, could floor his audience by the sheer brilliance of his thought and speech. His ideas were so crystal clear, fresh and appealing that there was no way to ignore him. In addition, he had a very good command over the language and could articulate his ideas very well. He seemed to have an answer for every question; every doubt of his disciples was clarified with utmost grace and ease. So much so that every discourse was fresh and original and all his discourses and thoughts were published as books. More than 600 books have been culled from his discourses. He was a speaker who became an author, as his ideas found a home in books.

Great orators and masters of rhetoric; the power of style

Oprah Winfrey, who has become rich and famous because of her oratorical skills, climbed up the ladder by her sheer ability to speak well. Born in rural poverty, she became a millionaire at the age of thirty-two with her talk show going national in the US.

Her popular talk show, 'The Oprah Winfrey Show', put her on the international podium. In 2004, she was the world's only black billionaire and world's first black woman billionaire in history with a net worth of $2.7 billion. She is a speaker first and billionaire later. She became rich and famous because of her oratorical skills and power to connect. She is a speaker who became a celebrity.

Speakers who made an impact with historical speeches; the power of substance

There have been times when historical speeches were made by people who were a part of the change; part of the making of history of their times. I must list a few of them because these speeches were, in the true sense, masterpieces of content, written in the context of those times.

Winston Churchill's historical address to the House of Commons during 1940, 'We will fight them on the beaches…', was delivered when the British armed forces and the allies were going through a very difficult time during the Second World War. Charles de Gaulle delivered a great speech, 'The appeal of

18th June' after the fall of France during the Second World War.

Some of the US Presidents gave momentous speeches befitting their times. John F. Kennedy's inaugural address to the nation, Ronald Reagan's 'Address to the Nation on the Challenges', and George Washington's 'Resignation Speech' are till date quoted by people.

Mahatma Gandhi's 'Quit India' speech was also very apt and hard-hitting.

Broadly, therefore, there are two types of speakers. First are those who are looked up to as 'sought-after' speakers because of what they have achieved in their life. For example, successful businessmen, authors, sportsmen or political figures. Then there are those who achieved success because of their philosophy, viewpoint and/or sheer ability to speak.

'The object of oratory alone is not truth, but persuasion'.
—William Bernbach

LESSONS FROM A BRILLIANT LEADER AND SPEAKER

- The great orators of ancient Rome and Greece—its philosophers and statesmen—proved the power of spoken word bringing about a golden age of eloquence, where philosophy and oratory converged. Mastering the art of oratory was essential to be considered an all-round individual those days.
- While public speaking focuses on conveying your point clearly and concisely, oratory is more persuasive and is intended to convince people. Oratory leans heavily on the emotional aspects of the context.
- The power of persuasion is one of the must-have abilities for leaders as well as managers. They have to be impressive and look convincing at board meetings, town hall meetings and brainstorming sessions. For politicians, being persuasive is essential and it is something that can either make or break them.
- The audience can be reached in two ways: first by an appeal to the intellect, and second, by an appeal to the emotions. Logic aims at the head while emotional appeals touch hearts. Brilliant speakers know exactly how to mix the two, according to their target audience. They are not merely reporters but are interpreters and analysts who make the audience view things from their perspective.
- There are several speakers who have the gift of the gab; they have a natural ability to speak brilliantly. There are many who are not gifted, but make colossal efforts to improve their oratorial skills. Many of them have become great speakers thanks to consistent efforts over a period of time.

- To become a great orator one has to have style, content and the ability to articulate. With practice all three can be mastered.
- Rhetoric is the art of persuasion, which can augment and boost the ability of writers and speakers to influence people. It is achieved by demonstrating great character, whipping up emotions and also making your audience feel that you are telling the truth.
- Great speakers can attain cult status and become celebrities by the sheer power of oratory. The reverse is also true, when celebrities also become sought-after speakers because of the status they have achieved in their respective fields.